1·2·3 Draw
Wild Animals

A step
by step
guide

by
Freddie
Levin

1·2·3 Draw
Wild Animals

A step
by step
guide

by
Freddie
Levin

Peel Productions, Inc.

Before you begin

You will need:

1. a pencil
2. an eraser
3. a pencil sharpener
4. lots of paper (recycle and re-use!)
5. colored pencils
6. a folder for saving work
7. a comfortable place to draw
8. good light

Now let's begin...!

Library of Congress Cataloging-in-Publication Data
Levin, Freddie.

1-2-3 draw wild animals: a step by step guide / by Freddie Levin. p. cm.
Includes index.
ISBN 0-939217-42-2 (paper: alk. paper)
1. Animals in art--Juvenile literature. 2. Wildlife art--Juvenile literature. 3. Drawing--Technique--Juvenile literature. [1. Animals in art. 2. Drawing--Technique.] I. Title: Wild animals. II. Title: One-two-three draw wild animals. III. Title.

NC780 .L44 2001 743.6--dc21   2001018530

Distributed to the trade and art markets in North America by

NORTH LIGHT BOOKS,
an imprint of F&W Publications, Inc.
4700 East Galbraith Road
Cincinnati, OH 45236

(800) 289-0963

Contents

Important drawing tip number 1:
*** Draw lightly at first, so you can erase extra lines. ***

Important drawing tip number 2:
*** Have fun drawing wild animals! ***

Important drawing tip number 3:
*** Practice, practice, practice and you **will** get better! ***

Circles, Ovals and Eggs

The drawings in this book start with three basic shapes:

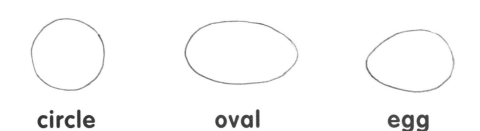

circle   **oval**   **egg**

*A circle is perfectly round.

*An oval is a squashed circle.

*An egg is an oval with one side fatter than the other.

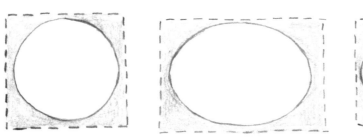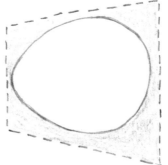

A **circle**   An **oval**   An **egg**
fits inside   fits inside   fits inside
a square.   a rectangle.   a trapezoid.

The more you practice drawing **circles**, **ovals**,
and **eggs**, the easier it will be.

Draw lightly!
Have fun!
Practice makes better!

4

Bush baby

1 Start with a **circle** and an **oval**. Notice how they overlap.

2 Draw two ears, two big googly eyes, and a U shape for the nose.

3 Draw a long curling tail. Draw small **oval** toes.

4 Draw lines inside each ear. Make small dashes for eyebrows. Add leg lines.

5 To finish the drawing, erase extra lines. Shade and color your bush baby. Give it a tree to sit in.

Bush babies are tiny tree-dwelling lemurs. They are nocturnal which means they are active at night. They are great leapers and their big googly eyes help them see in the dark. They eat insects, eggs, fruit and small animals.

Zebra

1 Start with a large **oval** and two **circles**: one small and one medium size. Notice the angles of the shapes and the distance between the three shapes.

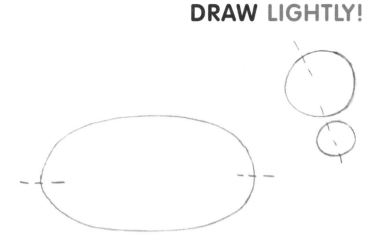

2 Connect the shapes with curved lines. Draw an ear and the beginning of a tail.

3 Draw an eye, nostril and mouth. Add the mane. Complete the tail. Draw the top sections of four legs.

6

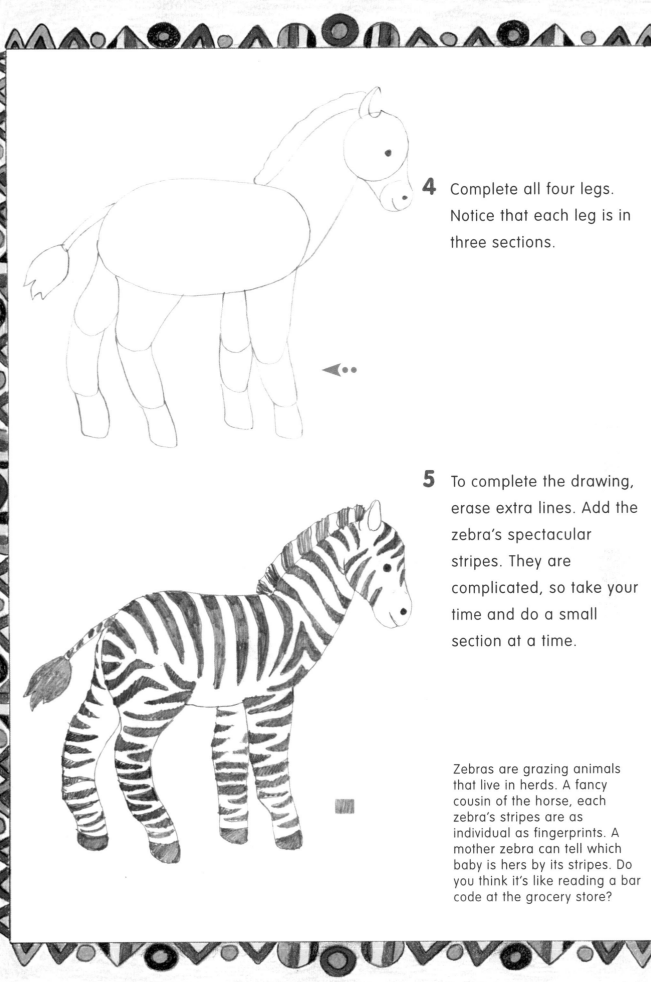

4 Complete all four legs. Notice that each leg is in three sections.

5 To complete the drawing, erase extra lines. Add the zebra's spectacular stripes. They are complicated, so take your time and do a small section at a time.

Zebras are grazing animals that live in herds. A fancy cousin of the horse, each zebra's stripes are as individual as fingerprints. A mother zebra can tell which baby is hers by its stripes. Do you think it's like reading a bar code at the grocery store?

Elephant

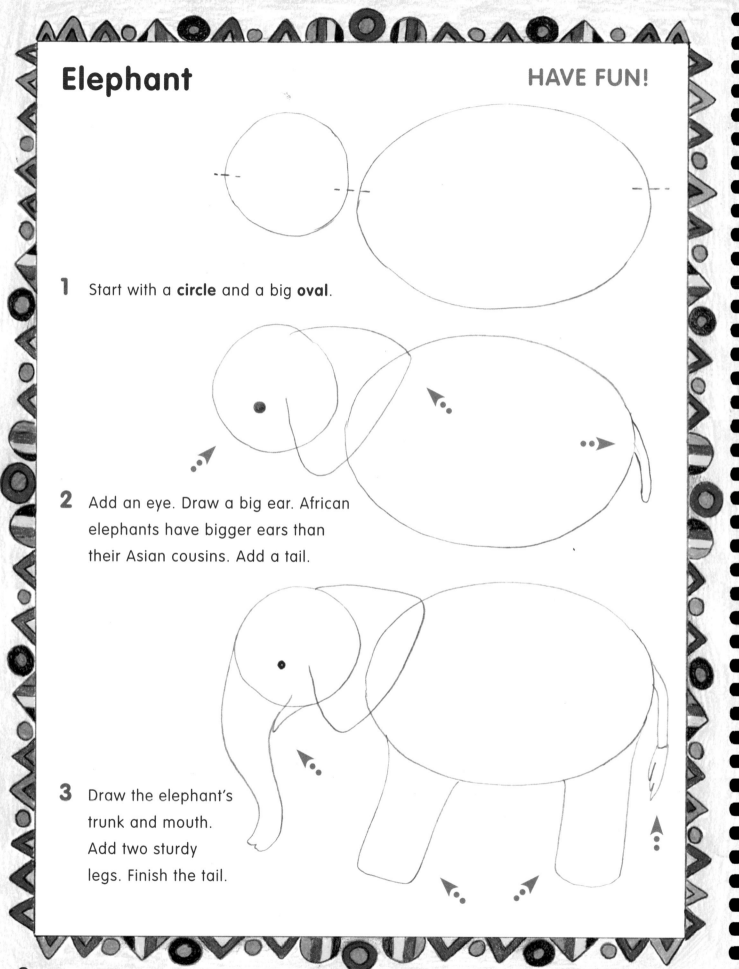

1 Start with a **circle** and a big **oval**.

2 Add an eye. Draw a big ear. African elephants have bigger ears than their Asian cousins. Add a tail.

3 Draw the elephant's trunk and mouth. Add two sturdy legs. Finish the tail.

Wild Animals from AFRICA

Elephants are the largest living land mammal. Mother elephants are pregnant for almost two years and baby elephants weigh around two hundred and fifty pounds at birth. Intelligent and social, they live in herds.

An elephant is the only animal with a trunk. Elephants use it to shower, carry food, cuddle a baby, sniff the wind, roll a heavy log, or greet a friend. When elephants meet each other, they put the tips of their trunks in each other's mouths.

4 Draw two more legs. Add a tusk.

5 To finish the drawing, erase extra lines. Add shading and color your elephant grey.

Excellent elephant!

Warthog

1 Start with a series of four **circles**. Draw the smallest lower than the others.

2 Carefully connect the **circles** with curved lines. Draw an eye and add the beginning of a tail.

3 Draw an **oval** with two small **circles** for the warthog's snout. Finish the tail. Draw two legs.

4 Draw ears. Add two more legs.

PRACTICE MAKES BETTER!

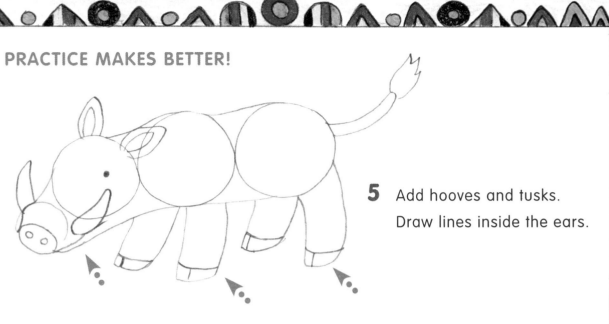

5 Add hooves and tusks. Draw lines inside the ears.

6 Draw a long bristly mane on the back and forehead.

7 To finish your drawing, erase extra lines. Shade your warthog and add color.

A warthog is a wild African pig. It lives in burrows, and likes to enter them backwards. Its tusks are used for digging and defense. The warthog diet consists of roots, eggs and small mammals.

Hippopotamus

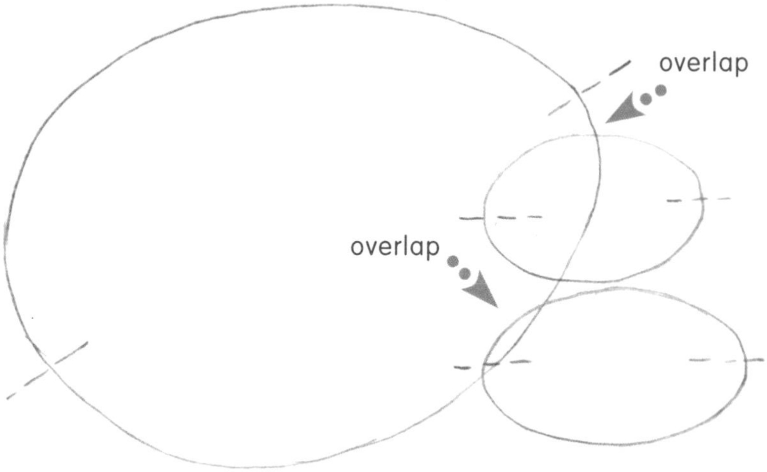

1 Start with a big **oval** and two smaller **ovals**. Notice how the two small **ovals** overlap the bigger one.

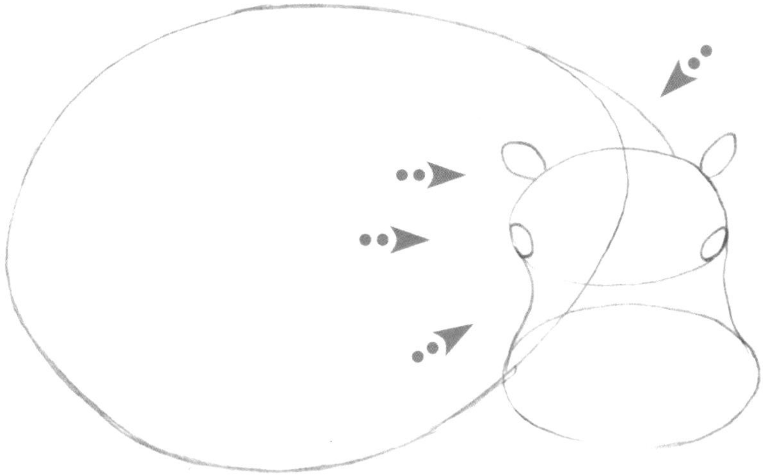

overlap

overlap

2 Connect the two smaller **ovals** with curved lines. Connect the head to the body with a curved line. Add two ears and eyes.

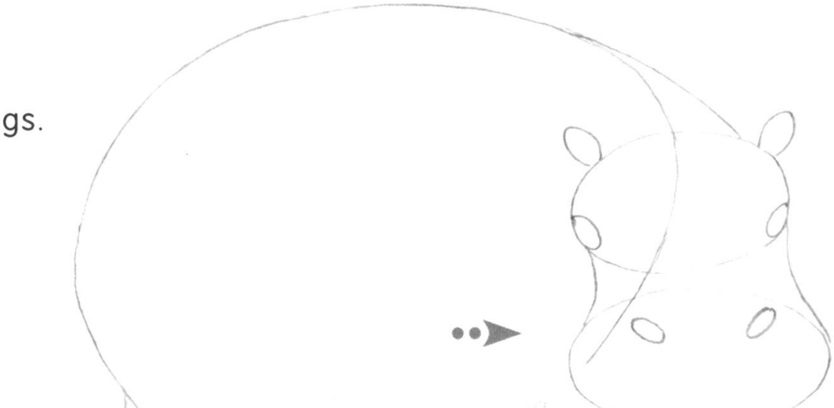

3 Draw nostrils. Add the lower jaw. Draw two legs.

4 Draw another front and rear leg. Add a squiggly tale. Complete the face and ears.

5 Erase extra lines. Shade and color your hippo.

Happy Hippo!

The name 'hippopotamus' means 'river horse' but the hippo is more hog than horse. It lives near water and spends much of its time submerged with only its eyes, ears and nostrils showing. A hippo calf can swim immediately after birth and often nurses underwater. Hippos eat mainly fruit, leaves and grass…a lot of it!

Lion

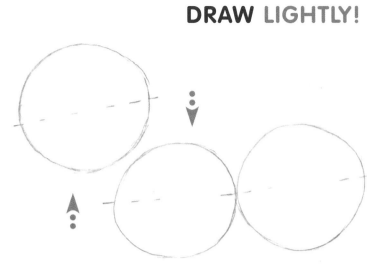

1 Draw three **circles**.
Notice their positions.

2 Use curved lines to
connect the neck and
body. Add ears, eyes and
a triangle nose.

3 Draw a mouth. Draw the
beginnings of the legs.
Add a tail.

14

4 Add the other rear leg. Draw the paws and finish the tail.

5 Erase the extra lines, shade and color. If it's a male lion, add a mane.

Adult male lions have a mane which grows in at around five to seven years old. Lions live in groups called prides. There is usually one male and several female lionesses plus the cubs. Lions eat mostly meat. The lionesses do most of the hunting and unless there are very young cubs, the male lion eats first.

Giraffe

1 Draw an **oval** and high above it, draw a smaller **oval**. (Can you guess why?)

2 Draw a small **circle** next to the small **oval**. Connect the head and body with two long neck lines. Draw a tail.

3 Draw curved lines to connect the circle and oval. Draw the mouth. Add an ear and a little horn. Start two legs.

4 Add another horn and lines inside the ear. Draw an eye and a nostril. Finish the tail. Draw more of the legs. Notice the round knee on the front leg.

Wild Animals from AFRICA

5 Add a mane. Complete the legs. Add the hoof sections.

6 Erase extra lines, add shading and color. The square brown spots of a giraffe are a bit complicated, so do a little section at a time. They help the giraffe blend with the trees and protect it from sharp-eyed enemies.

Giraffes are the tallest land animals. Their long neck and legs lets them eat leaves from the tops of the trees. The word 'giraffe' comes from the Arabic word 'zarafa' which means 'charming'. They have big dark eyes, little knobby horns and an eighteen inch dark blue tongue.

Wildebeest

1 Draw a small **egg** and a large **egg**. Notice the direction of each **egg**.

2 Add an eye. Draw curved lines to connect the head and body, and to flatten the back.

3 Draw nostrils and a small indent at the cheek. Draw two legs.

4 Draw two more legs. Add ears. Draw a second eye.

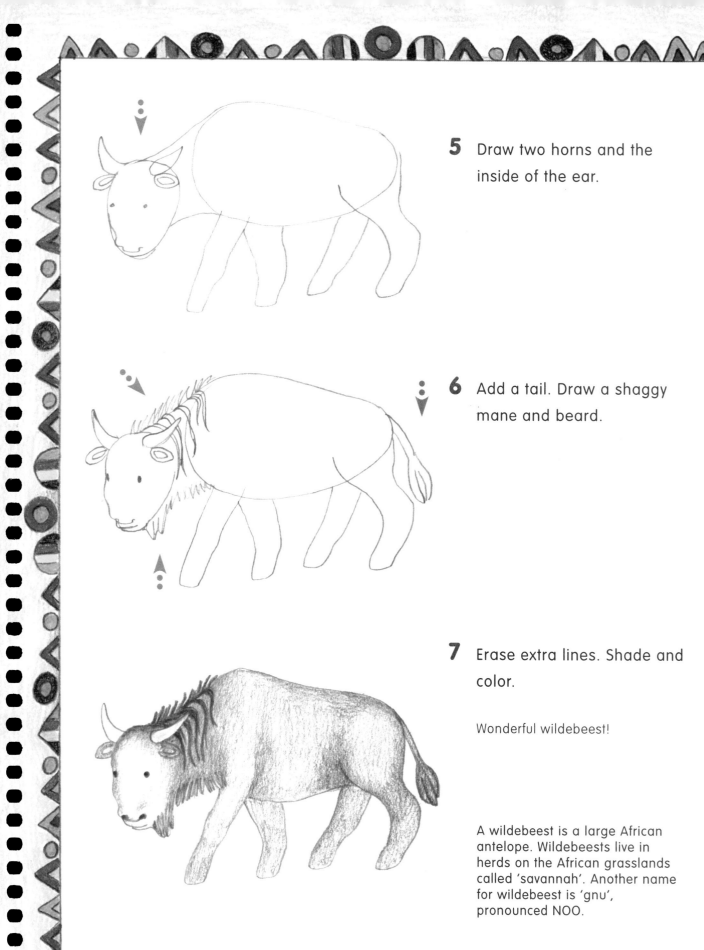

5 Draw two horns and the inside of the ear.

6 Add a tail. Draw a shaggy mane and beard.

7 Erase extra lines. Shade and color.

Wonderful wildebeest!

A wildebeest is a large African antelope. Wildebeests live in herds on the African grasslands called 'savannah'. Another name for wildebeest is 'gnu', pronounced NOO.

Panda

Pandas live in the bamboo forests that grow on upper mountain slopes in Southwest China and Tibet. They are extremely picky eaters— bamboo is the only food they eat!

1 Draw a vertical **egg** and put a **circle** on top of it.

2 Connect the neck and back with curving lines. Add two ears and two eyes.

3 Draw the front leg and paw in three sections. Add a triangle nose and a small upside-down 'T' for the mouth. Draw a **circle** to begin the hind leg.

4 Draw **circles** around the eyes and **half-circles** in the ears. Add curves where the other front paw and second hind leg will be.

5 Draw two back paws.

6 To finish the panda, erase extra lines and color. Give your panda some bamboo to eat.

The panda is an adorable looking animal that resembles a stuffed toy. The adults are almost six feet tall and the babies are a tiny five ounces. Pandas are not really bears but in a class all their own.

Tiger

1 Draw a **circle** for the head and an an **egg** for the body.

2 Connect the **circle** and the **egg** with two curving neck lines. Draw two round ears, two eyes and a triangle nose.

3 Draw the inside of the ears. Add the mouth. Draw two legs.

Tigers are the largest of the big cats. Unlike the sociable lion, tigers like to live alone. They hunt at night using their keen eyesight and although they don't climb very much, they are good swimmers. They are very adaptable and can live in many different climates from desert to swamp land.

4 Draw another front leg, another rear leg, and a tail.

5 Erase extra lines, shade and color. The tiger's beautiful stripes are a little complicated. Draw them a little at a time.

Terrific Tiger!

Orangutan

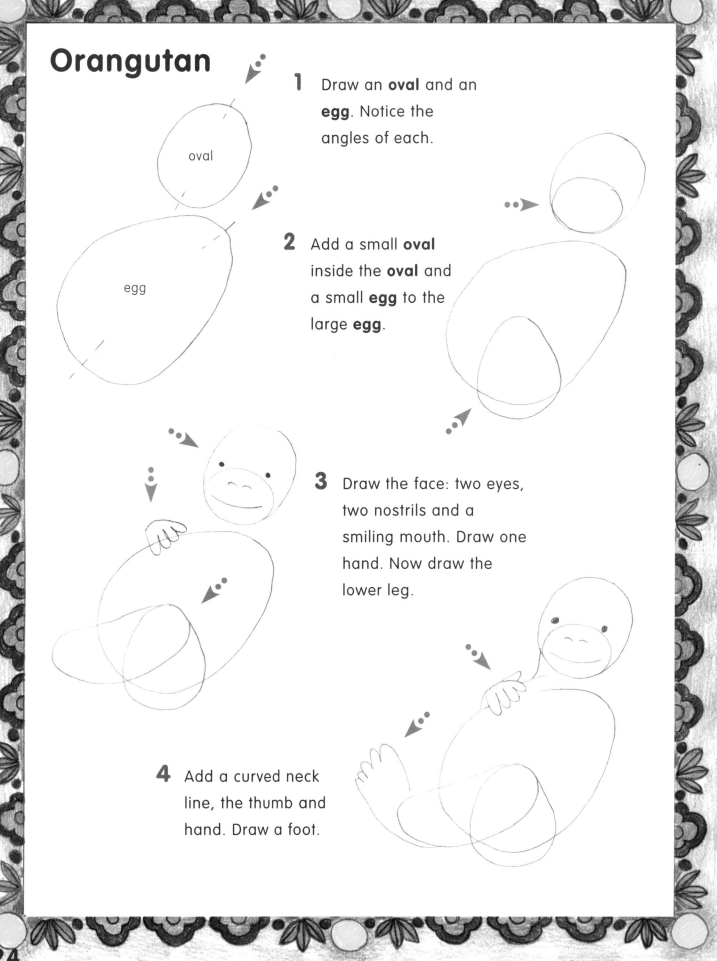

1 Draw an **oval** and an **egg**. Notice the angles of each.

oval

egg

2 Add a small **oval** inside the **oval** and a small **egg** to the large **egg**.

3 Draw the face: two eyes, two nostrils and a smiling mouth. Draw one hand. Now draw the lower leg.

4 Add a curved neck line, the thumb and hand. Draw a foot.

HAVE FUN!

5 Complete the other leg and foot. Draw a long stretched arm with fingers and a thumb.

6 To finish your drawing, erase the extra lines, shade and color. Use short pencil strokes to add fur.

Orangutans are large, red-haired, tree-dwelling apes from the rain forests of Borneo and Sumatra in Southeast Asia. Their name means 'man of the woods.' Orangutans are not as social as other apes and prefer to live alone. They make tree top nests woven out of branches and strip branches of leaves to use as simple tools. They are vegetarians.

Rhinoceros

Rhinos are relatively peaceful but can be very fierce when it comes to defending their babies. A baby rhinoceros is pink when it is born. Rhinos like to be near water and they like a good mud bath. They are relatives of horses and are vegetarians. A rhinoceros looks clumsy but it can run surprisingly fast.

1 Draw a small **egg** and a larger **oval**.

2 Add lines to form the head. Add an ear.

3 Draw lines to shape the shoulders and rump.

4 Draw another ear and a horn. Draw two sturdy legs. Begin the tail.

5 Add the nostril. Draw two more legs. Add toe nails. Finish the tail.

6 Erase extra lines. Shade and color.

Yak

1 Draw an **oval** and a small **egg**. Notice the angles of the shapes.

2 Draw lines to form the back and neck. Add an eye.

3 Add a line to shape the face. Draw two curving horns. Draw two legs.

The yak is the wild ox of Asia. It is larger than its domestic cousins.

4 Draw two more legs. Add a line for the nostrils.

5 Draw hooves. Add another eye.

6 Erase extra lines. Use long, light pencil strokes to make the yak shaggy. Finish coloring.

Yaks have thick woolly coats that can withstand the harsh mountain winds of the Himalayas. They are surprisingly agile and sure-footed on treacherous rocky paths. Yaks are almost six feet tall at the shoulder but carry their heads low, almost to the ground.

Armadillo

1 Draw an **oval** and a small **egg**. Notice the overlap and the angles of the shapes.

2 Add a line to shape the face. Draw a line for the neck. Add an eye.

3 Draw two ears. Draw lines to shape the bottom of the armadillo's body. Add two feet and a tail.

4 Draw the inside of the ear and the mouth. Add another leg. Draw curved lines on the back.

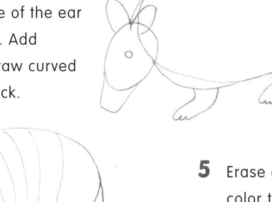

5 Erase extra lines. Shade and color the armadillo. Notice the markings and pattern of its 'armor.'

Insect-eating armadillos are nocturnal mammals that live in burrows in South and Central America and in some parts of the United States. Their leathery skin protects them. Some can also roll into a ball as a defense. Their funny, stiff gait makes them look a little like wind-up toys when they run.

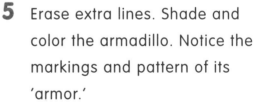

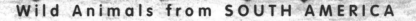

Jaguar

1 Draw a **circle** and an **egg**.

2 Add a curved line for the neck. Draw two ears. Draw two eyes and a triangle nose. Add a tail.

3 Draw the front legs. Draw lines in the ears. Draw a line for the mouth. Add a curved line for the top of the back leg. Add the lower back leg.

4 Erase extra lines, shade and color. Carefully fill in the jaguar's beautiful spots. Notice that they are not round like polka dots, but have an irregular shape.

The jaguar is the biggest member of the cat family in the Western Hemisphere. A jaguar is an agile climber and a night hunter. It will eat any kind of meat.

Tapir and her baby

Shy, forest dwelling tapirs resemble large pigs but they are more closely related to horses and rhinos. They like to live near water and are excellent swimmers. Tapirs eat roots, leaves, twigs and fruit. The babies are born with spots that disappear as they mature.

1 Draw a small **circle** and a large **oval**. (Do the same for the baby, only smaller.)

2 Draw curved neck lines, and a bulge for the snout (nose). Add a small tail.

3 Add lines to form the lower jaw. Add an eye, two ears, and two legs.

Wild Animals from SOUTH AMERICA

DRAW LIGHTLY!

4 Draw two more legs.

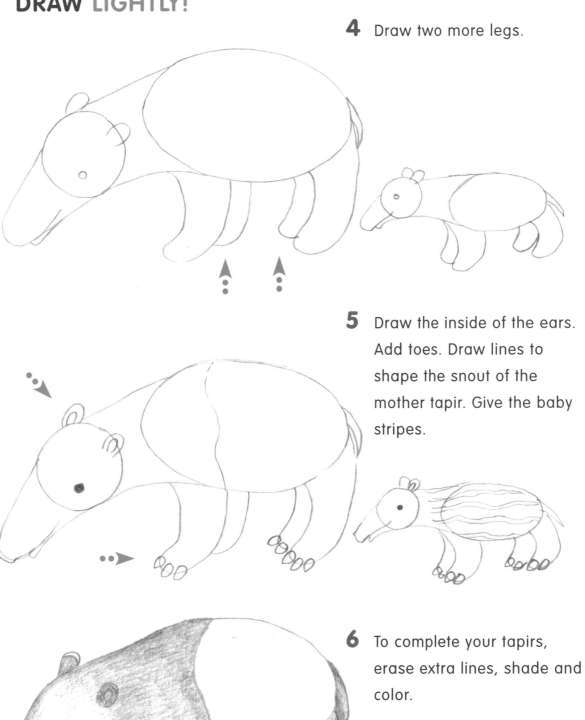

5 Draw the inside of the ears. Add toes. Draw lines to shape the snout of the mother tapir. Give the baby stripes.

6 To complete your tapirs, erase extra lines, shade and color.

Sloth

1 Draw an **oval** and an **egg**. Notice the angles.

2 Draw a neck line. Add two long limbs.

3 Draw two more legs. Draw the features of the face.

4 Add claws and a curving branch.

The sleepy, slow moving sloth spends most of its time hanging upside down from tree branches. It rarely comes down, finding all of the twigs, leaves and moisture it needs high up above the ground. It even sleeps that way.

5 Erase extra lines, shade and color. To make him shaggy, use short light pencil strokes.

Super sloth!

Guanaco

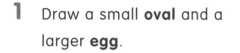

1 Draw a small **oval** and a larger **egg**.

2 Add lines to form the face. Add a nostril, eye and ear. Draw curving neck lines.

3 Add another ear. Draw the tail. Draw two legs. Notice how the legs are divided into sections.

4 Draw two more legs. Add lines to the ears.

5 To complete the guanaco, erase extra lines, shade and color. Short light pencil strokes will make it look woolly.

Great Guanaco!

The guanaco is the wild cousin of the domesticated llama. Llamas, vicuñas, alpacas and guanacos are in the camel family. Guanacos live in the plains and mountains of South America. Its woolly coat is reddish brown and white. A baby guanaco is called a 'chulengo'.

Anteater

1 Draw a big **oval** and a small **oval**. Notice the angle of the small **oval**.

2 Draw curving neck lines and a l-o-o-o-ng nose. Add an eye and an ear.

3 Draw the other ear and a nostril. Draw three legs.

Wild Animals from SOUTH AMERICA

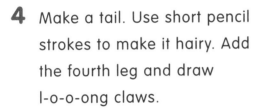

4 Make a tail. Use short pencil strokes to make it hairy. Add the fourth leg and draw l-o-o-ong claws.

5 Erase extra lines, shade and color. Note the markings on the anteater's side. Draw some ants for your anteater.

The anteater has nine inch claws and a long tube shaped head. It is perfectly adapted for ripping open nests and scooping up ants and termites with its tongue. The anteater is almost six feet long but its mouth is only one inch wide. It lives in the tropical forests and grassy plains of South America.

Peccary

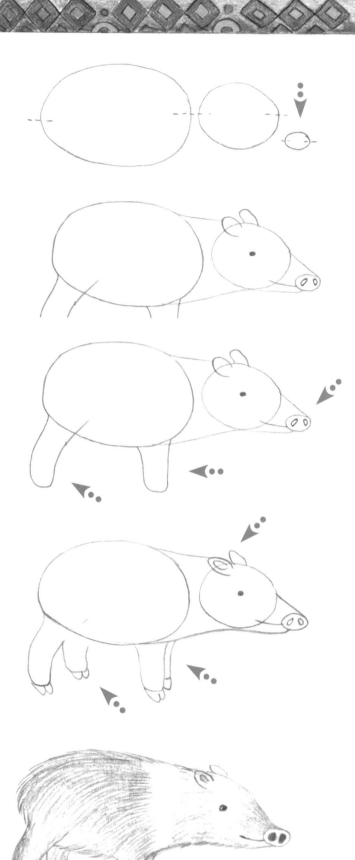

1 Draw a large **oval**, a smaller **oval** and a really small **oval**. Notice the position of the three **ovals**.

2 Draw lines for the neck, and two ears. Add an eye.

3 Draw lines to form the face. The smallest **oval** becomes the snout. Add two nostrils. Draw a mouth. Add two legs.

4 Draw two more legs and add hooves. Draw lines inside the ear.

5 Erase extra lines, shade and color. To make the bristly fur, use short, light pencil strokes.

The peccary is a wild pig. It lives mostly on roots and berries. It is shy and timid unless attacked. Another name for a peccary is a ' javeline.'

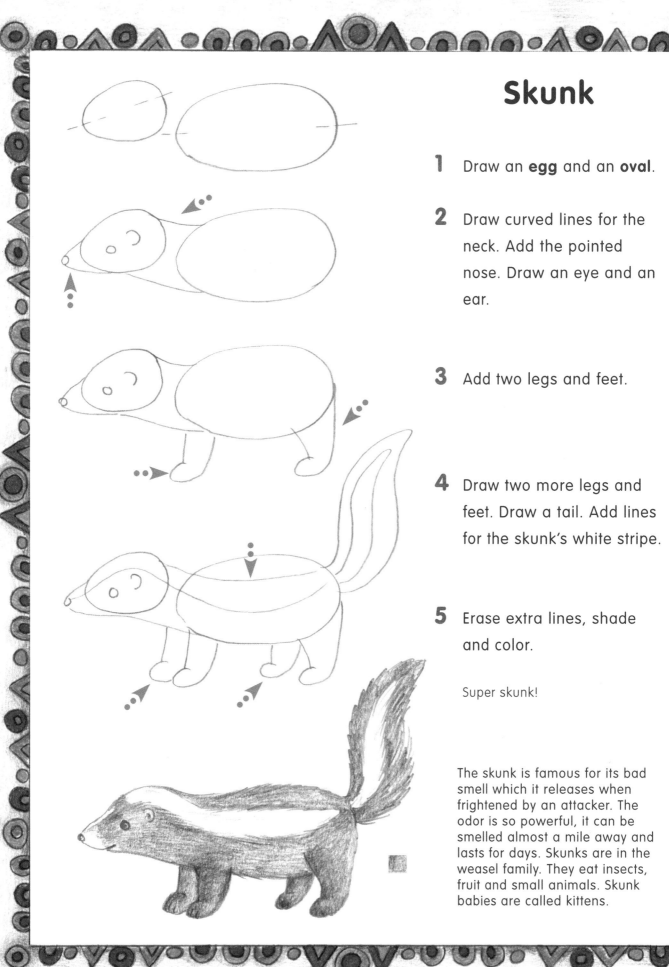

Skunk

1 Draw an **egg** and an **oval**.

2 Draw curved lines for the neck. Add the pointed nose. Draw an eye and an ear.

3 Add two legs and feet.

4 Draw two more legs and feet. Draw a tail. Add lines for the skunk's white stripe.

5 Erase extra lines, shade and color.

Super skunk!

The skunk is famous for its bad smell which it releases when frightened by an attacker. The odor is so powerful, it can be smelled almost a mile away and lasts for days. Skunks are in the weasel family. They eat insects, fruit and small animals. Skunk babies are called kittens.

Raccoon

1 Draw a large **egg** overlapping a smaller **egg**. Notice the angle of both.

overlap

2 Add two ears, two eyes, and a nose.

3 Draw front legs and paws.

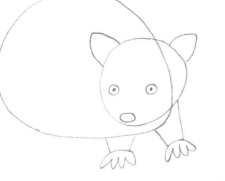

4 Draw a back leg and a big tail.

Wild Animals from NORTH AMERICA

5 Draw the face markings. Draw the inside of the ears. Draw stripes on the tail. Add a line to shape the stomach.

6 Add lines around the eyes.

7 To complete the raccoon, erase extra lines, shade and draw.

Raccoons have striped tails and black masks that make them look like little bandits. They are comfortable on the ground and in trees and prefer to make their homes in dens. They have skillful little paws that they can use almost like hands. Raccoons that live near people can be pests because they like to look for dinner in your garbage can.

Bighorn Sheep

DRAW LIGHTLY!

1 Draw a big **egg** and a small **egg**. Notice the angles.

2 Add lines to form the face. Draw an eye. Add curving lines for the neck.

3 Draw the markings around the nose. Add two legs. Draw the tail and markings around it.

Wild Animals from NORTH AMERICA

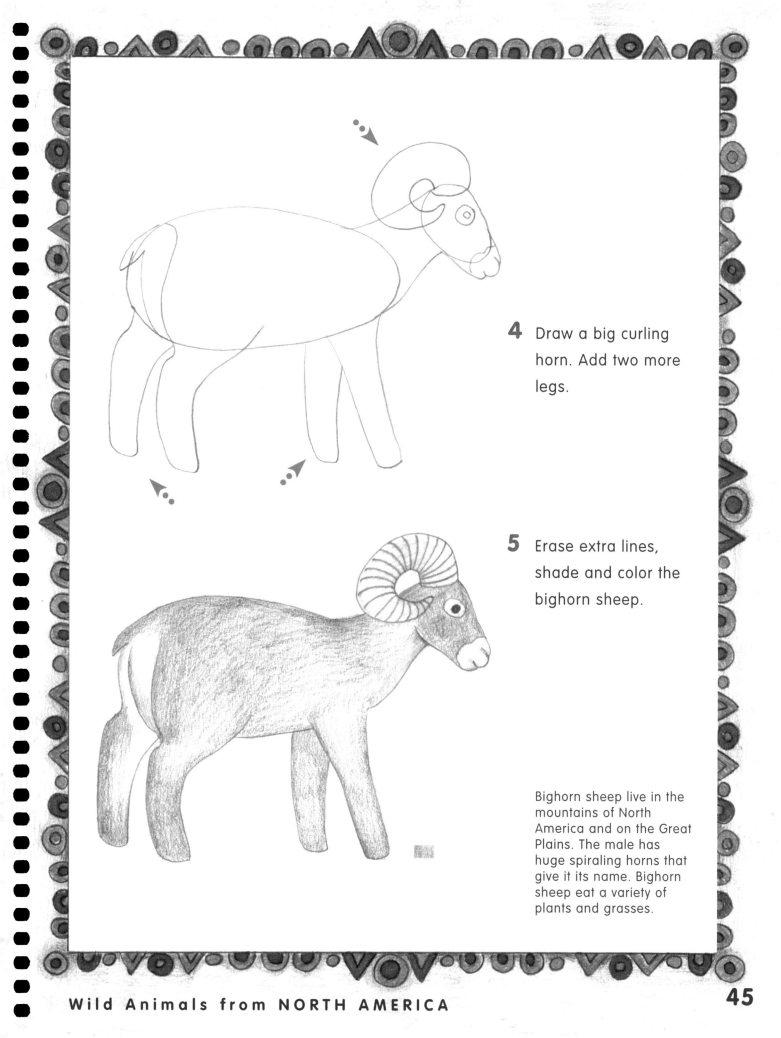

4 Draw a big curling horn. Add two more legs.

5 Erase extra lines, shade and color the bighorn sheep.

Bighorn sheep live in the mountains of North America and on the Great Plains. The male has huge spiraling horns that give it its name. Bighorn sheep eat a variety of plants and grasses.

Prairie dog

1 Draw a skinny, vertical **egg**. Above it draw a small **egg**. Notice the angle.

2 Draw lines to form the nose. Add an eye. Draw curving neck lines.

3 Draw an ear. Add a front paw and a back leg.

4 Draw another back leg. Add a curving line to shape the stomach.

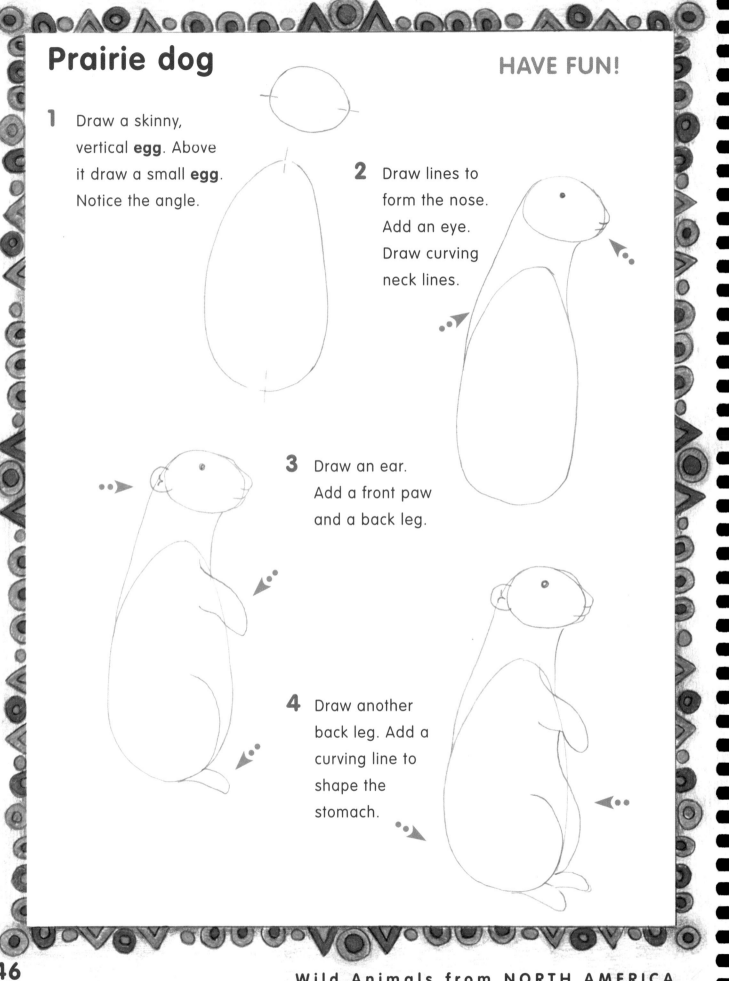

5 Add a second front paw. Draw a tail.

6 Erase extra lines, shade and color. Make your prairie dog guarding the entrance to a burrow.

Prairie dogs are not dogs. They are relatives of squirrels. The name comes from its short, sharp bark. Prairie dogs are highly social animals and live in a community of connecting tunnels and burrows that is called a 'city'.

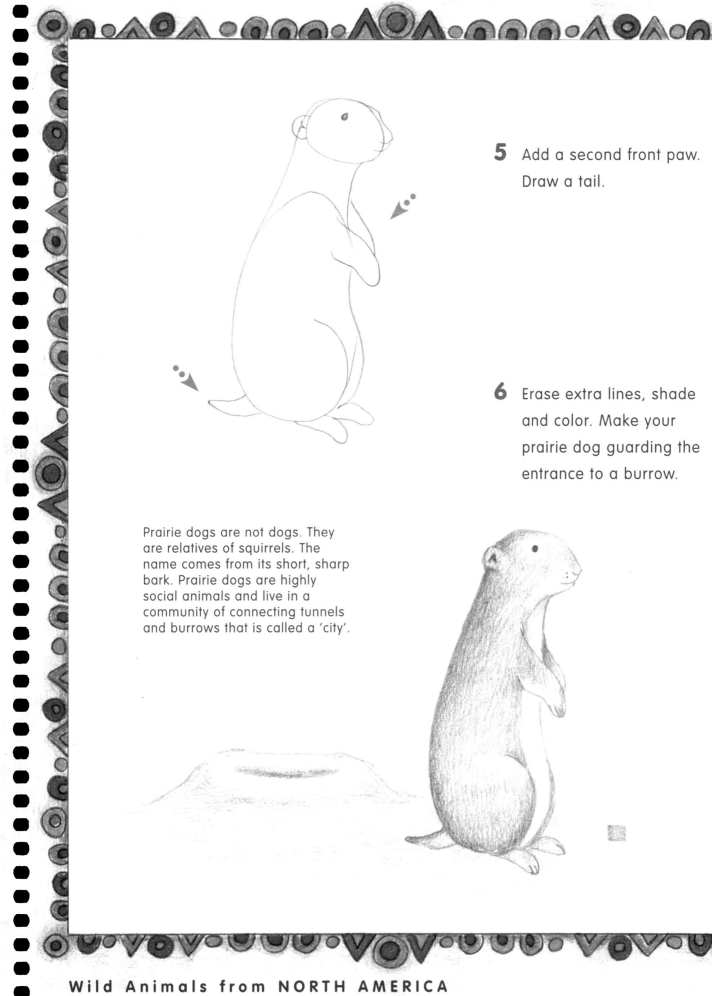

Bison (buffalo)

1 Draw a large **egg** and a
small **egg**. Notice the
position of both shapes.

2 Draw a curved line for the
back of the neck. Draw an
eye. Add two legs.

3 Add two horns. Draw the
shaggy clump of hair on
the bison's forehead. Add
an ear. Draw the nose.
Draw two more legs.

Wild Animals from NORTH AMERICA

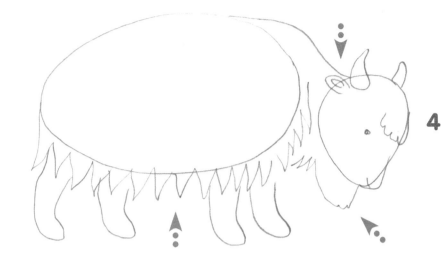

4 Draw the bison's shaggy fur. Make his shaggy beard. Draw the inside of the ear.

5 To complete your bison, erase extra lines, shade and color.

Beautiful bison!

The American bison is also commonly called a buffalo. Huge herds once roamed the plains from the Appalachian mountains to the western Rockies. They were an important part of the Native American way of life as a source of food, clothing and hides for shelters. In the 1800's, they were hunted almost to extinction, but with careful conservation, their numbers have increased.

Wolf

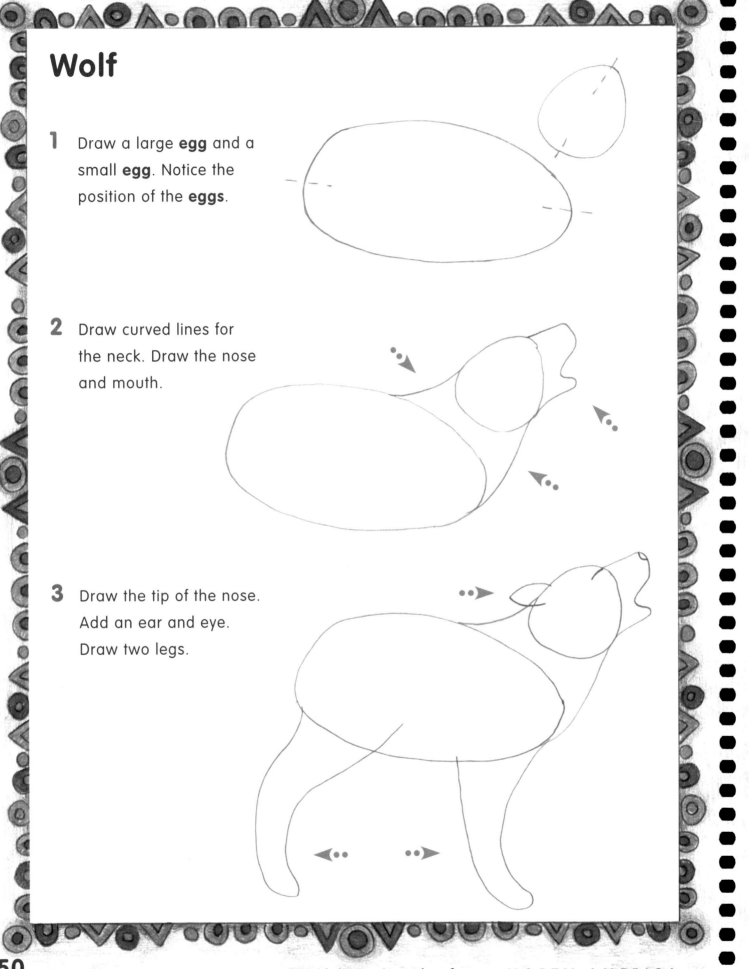

1 Draw a large **egg** and a small **egg**. Notice the position of the **eggs**.

2 Draw curved lines for the neck. Draw the nose and mouth.

3 Draw the tip of the nose. Add an ear and eye. Draw two legs.

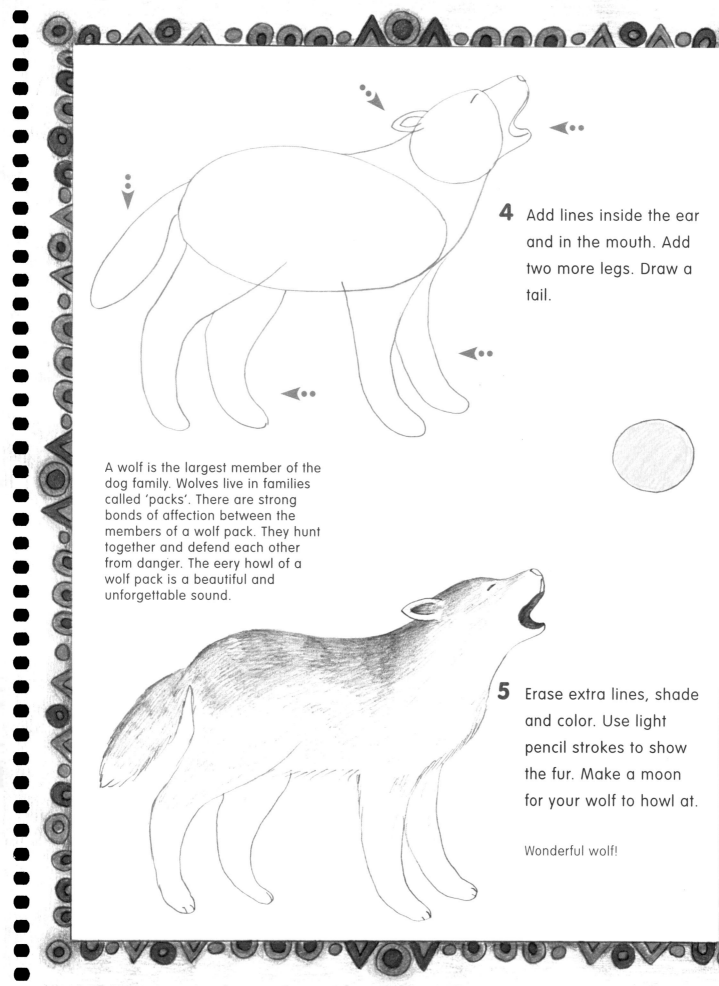

4 Add lines inside the ear and in the mouth. Add two more legs. Draw a tail.

A wolf is the largest member of the dog family. Wolves live in families called 'packs'. There are strong bonds of affection between the members of a wolf pack. They hunt together and defend each other from danger. The eery howl of a wolf pack is a beautiful and unforgettable sound.

5 Erase extra lines, shade and color. Use light pencil strokes to show the fur. Make a moon for your wolf to howl at.

Wonderful wolf!

Deer

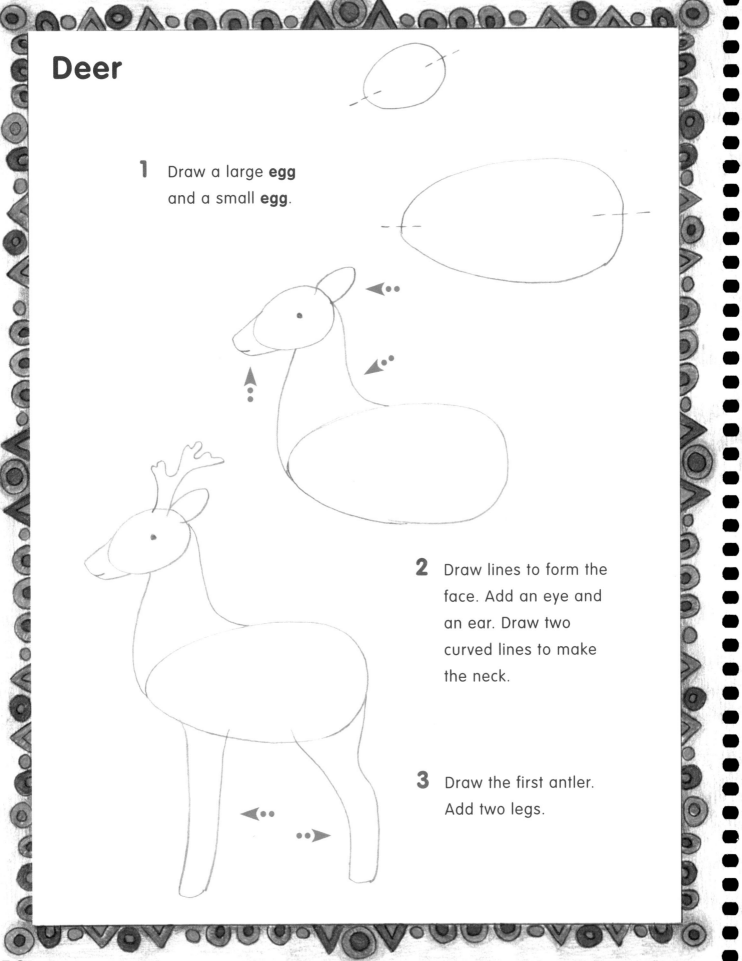

1 Draw a large **egg** and a small **egg**.

2 Draw lines to form the face. Add an eye and an ear. Draw two curved lines to make the neck.

3 Draw the first antler. Add two legs.

DRAW LIGHTLY!

4 Draw the second antler. Add lines to the ear and eye. Outline the white patch on the deer's chest. Draw a line for the stomach. Add two more legs. Draw hooves and a tail.

5 Erase extra lines, shade and color.

The deer family, which includes moose, caribou and elk, are the only animals that have bones on their heads called antlers. (Antlers are very different from horns.) Usually it is only the male that has them. Most deer shed their antlers every year and grow a new pair in the spring.

Kangaroo

1 Draw a small **egg** and a large **egg**.

2 Draw lines to form the face. Add an eye and a nostril. Draw an **oval** for the upper arm. Make a line for the kangaroo's pouch.

3 Draw two ears. Add the lower arm. Draw a tiny **oval** above the line of the pouch for the head of the kangaroo's joey. Add a curved line to start the hind leg.

Wild Animals from **AUSTRALIA**

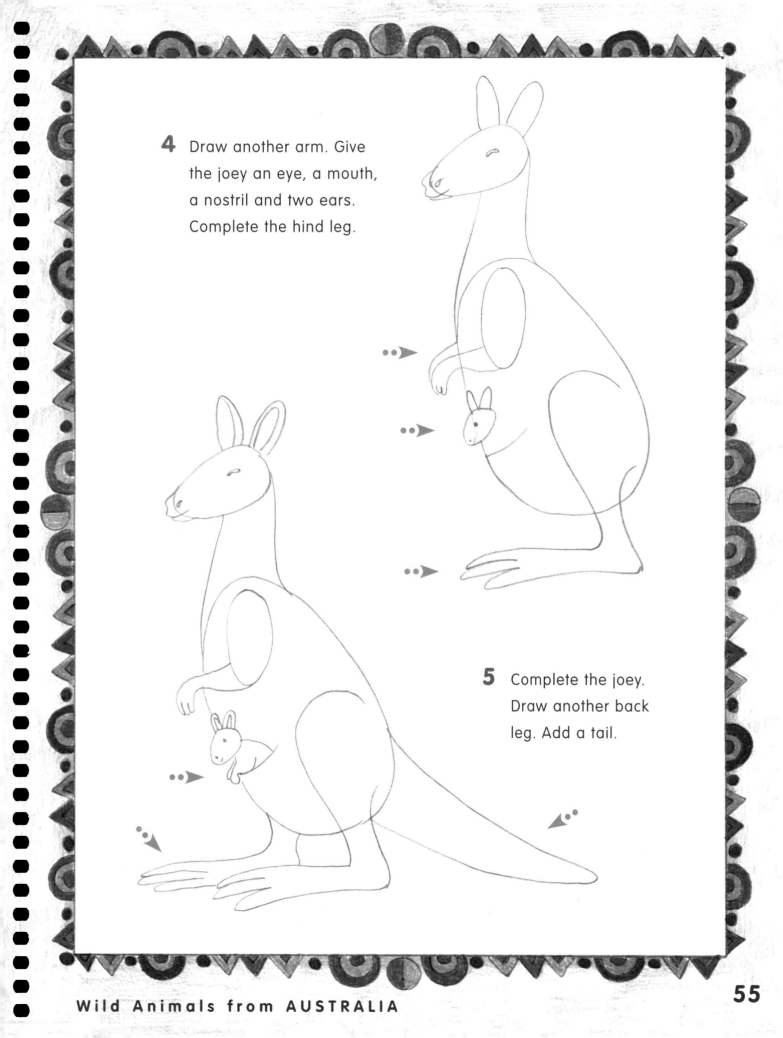

4 Draw another arm. Give the joey an eye, a mouth, a nostril and two ears. Complete the hind leg.

5 Complete the joey. Draw another back leg. Add a tail.

6 To complete your kangaroos, erase extra lines, shade and color.

Kangaroos are marsupials. This means that after their babies are born, they live in their mother's pouch until they are old enough to get around on their own. A baby kangaroo is called a 'joey'. Kangaroos are almost six feet tall. They eat grass and plants and travel in large groups called 'mobs'.

Platypus

1 Draw an **egg**. Notice the angle.

2 Add a tail and two legs. Draw two eyes. Add lines to begin the duck like bill.

3 Draw the platypus' duck bill. Add another front leg.

4 Erase extra lines, shade and color.

Pretty Platypus!

The platypus is a mixed-up looking animal. It is one of only two egg-laying mammals (the other is the echidna). It has webbed feet and a snout that looks like a duck's bill. The platypus lives in burrows along Australian streams where it catches small shellfish, worms and grubs. It's about two feet long and only weighs about five pounds. Its fur makes it appear larger.

Wombat

1 Draw a big **circle** and a smaller **circle**.

2 Draw two curved lines for the neck. Draw the face. Add an eye.

3 Draw two legs. Add an ear.

4 Draw a line inside the ear. Add another ear. Draw a nose. Draw two more legs.

5 Erase extra lines, shade and color.

Wonderful wombat!

A wombat is a short, stocky burrowing animal. It is nocturnal, which means it is active at night. It lives on grasses and roots. The wombat is a marsupial, and its pouch faces backwards, (the opposite of the kangaroo) so that as it digs, the flying dirt does not disturb its babies.

Koala

Koalas look like bears but they're not. These sleepy marsupials spend most of their lives in the fork of a eucalyptus tree, eating its leaves and shoots. They get all the moisture they need from the leaves. Their name, koala, is an Australian Aborigine word meaning 'no drink'.

1 Draw an **egg** and a **circle**. Notice how they overlap.

2 Draw two ears, two eyes and a triangle nose.

3 Add a triangle to the nose and a little upside down 'T'. Draw the front leg.

4 Draw lines inside the ears. Add two little eyebrows. Draw the back leg. Add claws.

5 Erase extra lines, shade and color. Put your koala in its favorite place: a eucalyptus (yoo-ka-LIP-tus) tree.

Cute koala!

Polar bear

1 Draw a big **oval** and a small **circle**.

2 Draw the face. Add two ears and an eye. Add curved lines for the neck.

3 Draw two legs.

4 Draw a nose and the inside of the ear. Add another front leg and a curved line for the other rear leg.

5 To complete your polar bear, erase extra lines, shade and color.

Perfect Polar Bear!

Polar bears are large white bears that live where it is very cold. They have heavy coats and thick layers of fat to keep them warm. Polar bears have varied diets. They eat meat, fish, berries and grasses.

Walrus

1 Start with a big **egg** and a small **circle**.

2 Draw a second **egg** around the small **circle**.

overlap

3 Add two curved lines for the neck and stomach. Add two eyes and a nose. Begin the rear flipper.

PRACTICE MAKES BETTER!

4 Finish the rear flipper. Draw lines for the muzzle underneath the walrus' nose.

5 Add two tusks. Draw two front flippers.

The walrus is a 'pinniped' which means that their feet, like a seal's, are flippers. Walruses are huge - up to fifteen feet long and over three thousand pounds. Their fat keeps them warm in the cold Arctic waters. They eat mostly clams and other shellfish. Walruses use their tusks as a weapon for defense, as a tool for digging up food and as a hook for climbing.

6 Erase extra lines, shade and color.

Index

Learn about other drawing books online at **1-2-3-draw.com!**

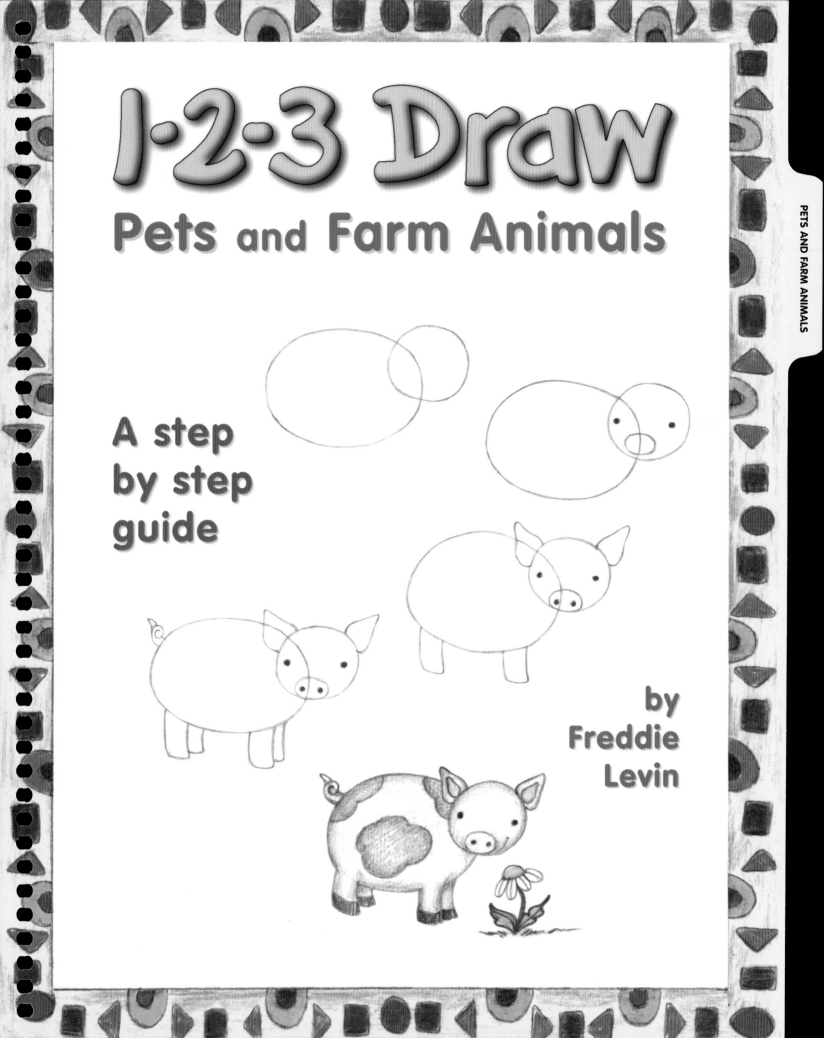

1·2·3 Draw

Pets and Farm Animals

A step
by step
guide

by
Freddie
Levin

1·2·3 Draw

Pets and Farm Animals

A step
by step
guide

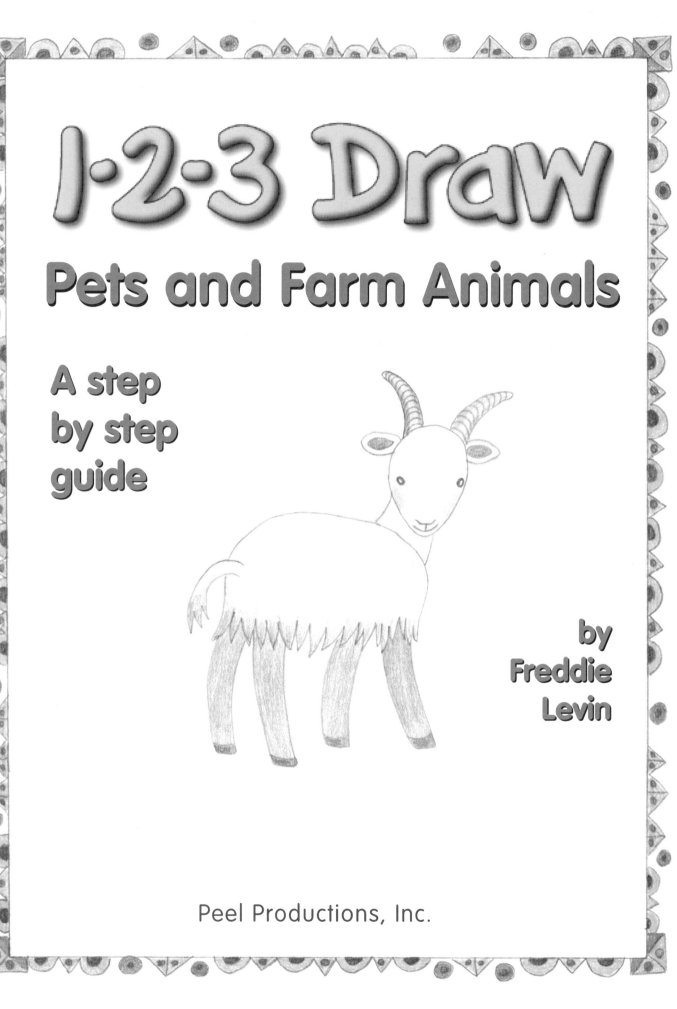

by
Freddie
Levin

Peel Productions, Inc.

Before you begin

You will need:

1. a pencil

2. an eraser

3. a pencil sharpener

4. lots of paper (recycle and re-use!)

5. colored pencils

6. a folder for saving work

7. a comfortable place to draw

8. good light

Now let's begin...!

Library of Congress Cataloging-in-Publication Data

Levin, Freddie.
    1-2-3 draw pets and farm animals / by Freddie Levin.
        p. cm.
    Includes index.
    ISBN 0-939217-40-6
        1. Domestic animals in art--Juvenile literature. 2. Drawing--Technique--Juvenile
literature. [1. Domestic animals in art. 2. Animals in art. 3. Drawing--Technique.] I.
Title: One-two-three draw pets and farm animals. II. Title.

NC783.8.D65 L48 2000

743.6--dc21   00-055072

Distributed to the trade and art
markets in North America by

NORTH LIGHT BOOKS,
an imprint of F&W Publications, Inc.
4700 East Galbraith Road
Cincinnati, OH 45236

(800) 289-0963

Contents

Important drawing tip number 1:

*** Draw lightly at first, so you can erase extra lines ***

Important drawing tip number 2:

*** Have fun drawing pets and farm animals! ***

Important drawing tip number 3:

*** Practice makes better ***

Circles, ovals and eggs

The drawings in this book start with three basic shapes:

circle   **oval**   **egg**

*A circle is perfectly round.

*An oval is a squashed circle.

*An egg is an oval with one side fatter than the other.

A **circle**
fits inside
a square.

An **oval**
fits inside
a rectangle.

An **egg**
fits inside
a trapezoid.

The more you practice drawing **circles**, **ovals** and
eggs, the easier it will be.

Remember:
Draw lightly!

1 Draw a **circle** and an **egg**.

2 Connect them with two curved lines.

3 Add triangle ears and two legs.

4 Add two more legs and a tail.

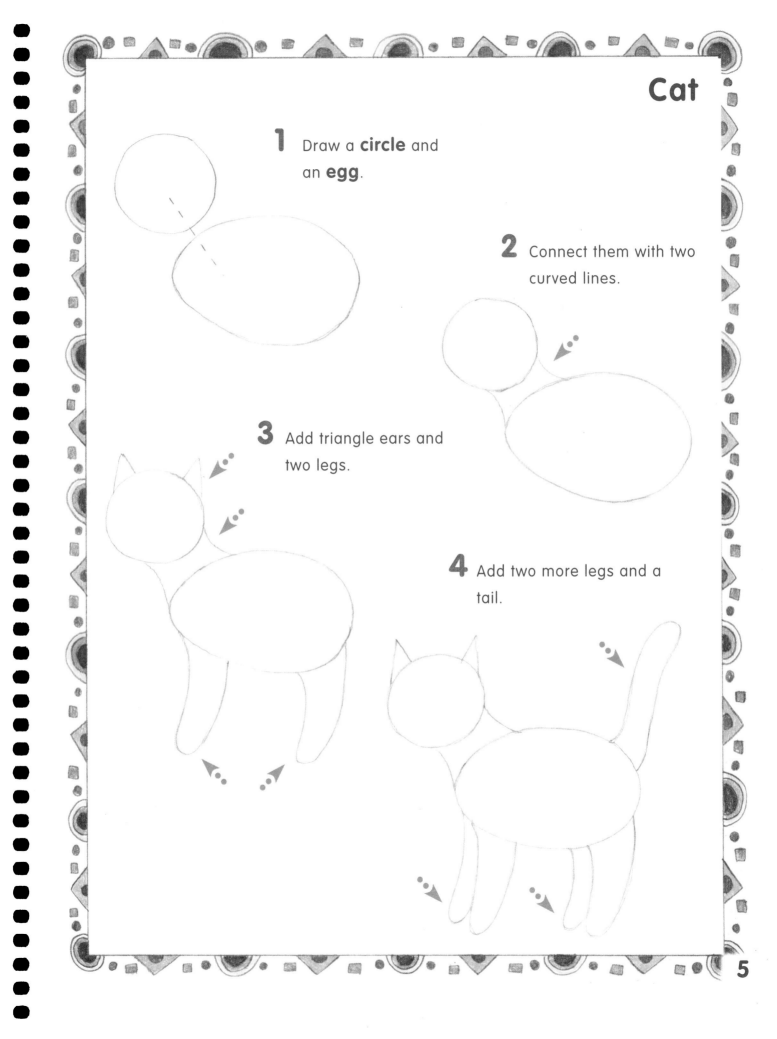

5 Add two eyes and
a triangle nose.

6 Erase the extra lines.

7 Draw a mouth and
whiskers. Add stripes.
Color your cat.

A cat can be a great pet.
Cats like to cuddle and
play. When they are happy,
you can hear them purr.

Sitting cat

1 Draw a **circle** above an **egg**.

2 Add triangle ears. Draw two front legs.

3 Add eyes, a triangle nose and a mouth.

Add small back feet.

4 Draw whiskers. Add a tail. Shade ears. Erase extra lines!

About cats

Spotted cats are called **Calico cats**.

Striped cats are called **Tabby cats**.

This cat is a **Scaredy cat!**

1 2 3

Draw a catnip mouse for **your** cat!

Dog

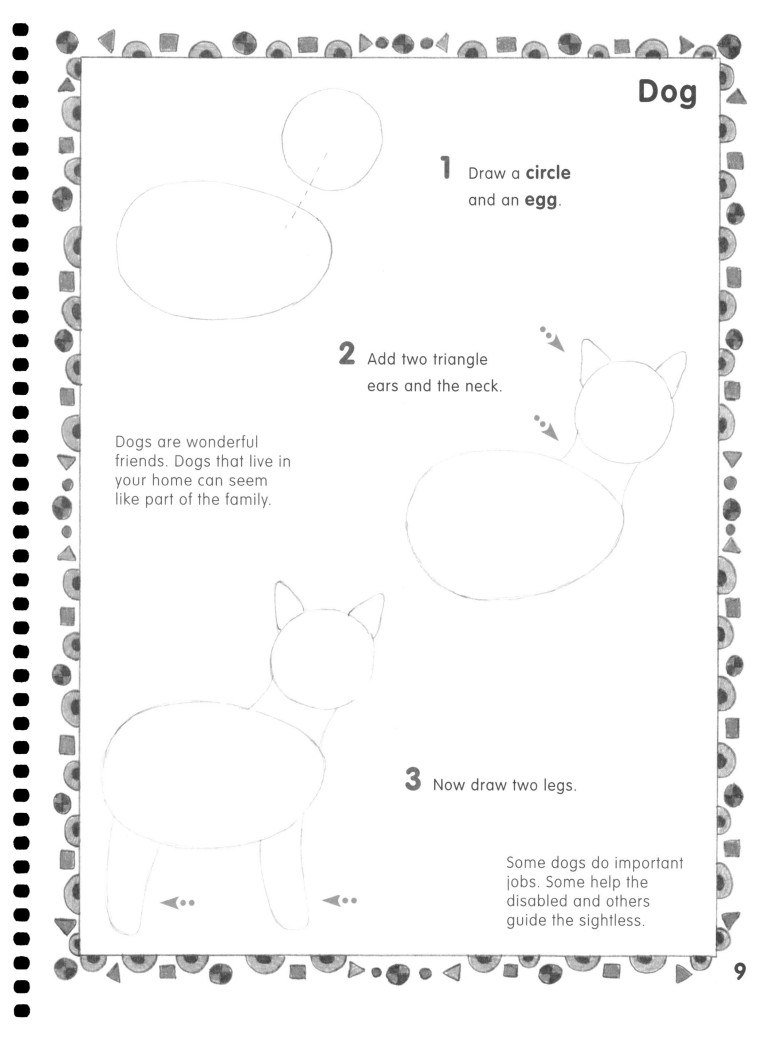

1 Draw a **circle** and an **egg**.

2 Add two triangle ears and the neck.

Dogs are wonderful friends. Dogs that live in your home can seem like part of the family.

3 Now draw two legs.

Some dogs do important jobs. Some help the disabled and others guide the sightless.

4 Draw a stubby tail. Add two eyes, and two more legs.

5 Add lines for the markings on the face and legs. Draw a nose and a mouth.

6 Erase extra lines and shade dark areas. Draw a collar for your dog.

This dog looks ready to play ball. Draw a ball and a rubber bone for your dog.

Sitting dog

1 Draw a **circle** above an **egg**. Notice that they **overlap**.

2 Add two floppy ears. Draw two eyes.

3 Draw a triangle nose. Add two front paws.

4 Draw the mouth and back legs.

5 Shade ears. Draw lines for toes. Erase extra lines and color your dog.

Good dog!

Rabbit

1 Start with a **circle** on top of an **egg.**

2 Draw two long ears and two eyes.

3 Add a nose, front feet, back feet, and a tail.

4 Draw a mouth. Add lines for toes, and make the tail fluffy. Erase extra lines. Add color.

Idea!
Make a carrot for your rabbit.

Another rabbit

1 Draw a **circle** on top of an **egg.**

2 Add one ear, one eye. and a fluffy tail.

3 Add another ear and a nose. Draw two feet.

4 Put lines in the ears and draw a mouth. Draw another front foot.

5 Erase extra lines and add color!

A rabbit can be a peaceful, gentle pet.

Parakeet

1 Start with a **circle** and an **egg.**

2 Draw a circle for the eye. Connect the head and body with curved lines.

Add the flight feathers.

3 Draw a beak. Shade the eye. Add a tail. Draw two feet.

4 Draw stripes on the head and wings. Add dots near the beak. Color the tummy, tail and beak.

Lively, colorful parakeets are the most popular pet bird. With patience and gentle handling, they can become very tame, learn tricks and even speak a few words.

5 Erase extra lines. Give your parakeet a perch.

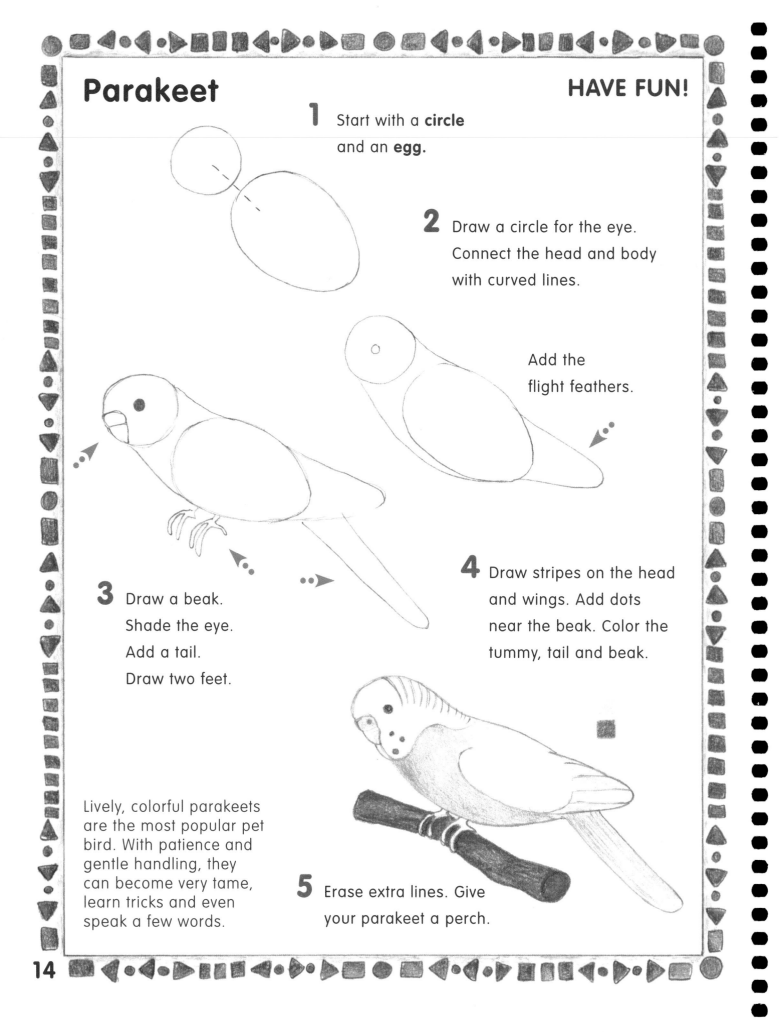

14

Canary

1 Draw a **circle** and **egg**. Make them **overlap**.

2 Add a wing shape.

3 Draw an eye and a pointy beak.

4 Now draw a tail and two feet.

5 Erase extra lines and give your bird a perch. Color your canary.

Canaries have been kept as pets for hundreds of years. Male canaries have a beautiful rolling song.

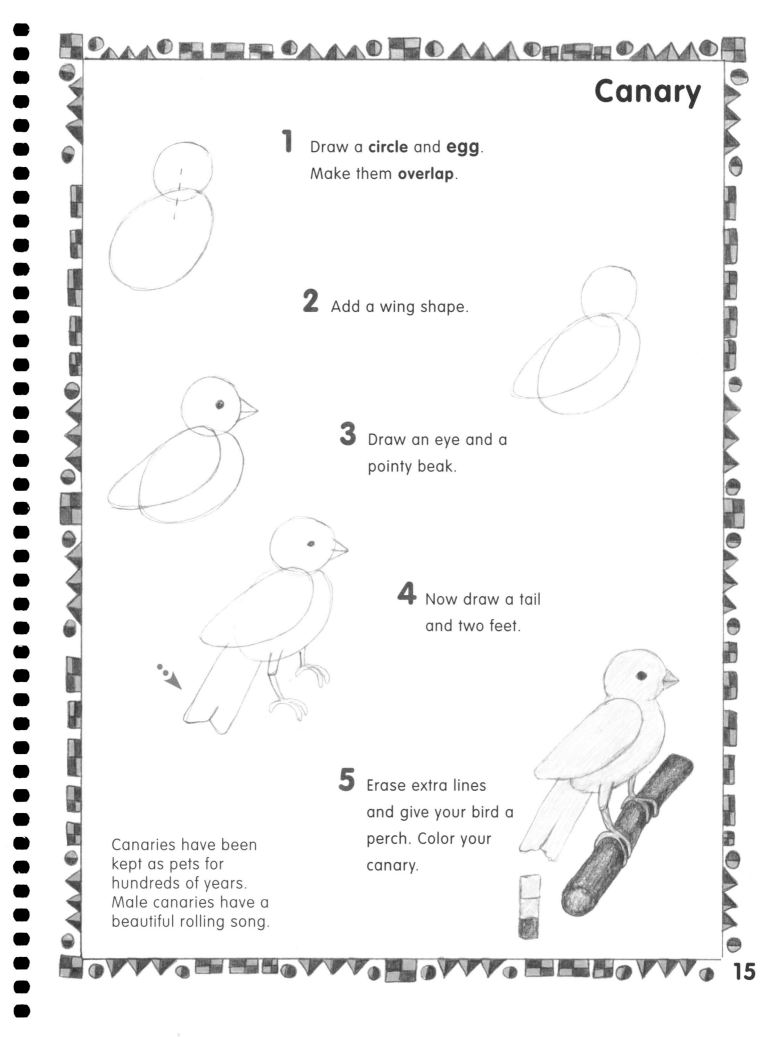

Parrot

1 Start with a **circle** and an **egg**.

2 Add an eye and two curved lines for a neck.

3 Add a curved upper beak. Add wing feathers.

4 Draw the lower beak. Add tail feathers.

Parrots come in every color of the rainbow. They range in size from tiny parrotlets to great big macaws.

Parrots need special care to stay healthy and happy. They have long life spans. Some parrots can live fifty or sixty years.

5 Add the bump on a parrot's nose called a cere. Add feet.

6 Erase extra lines. Add shading and color the feathers. Add feather lines on wings and tail. Draw a perch for your parrot.

Many parrots are very intelligent. Parrots are well-known for their ability to mimic human speech.

Mouse

1 Draw a small **egg** and a large **egg**. Notice the angle of both.

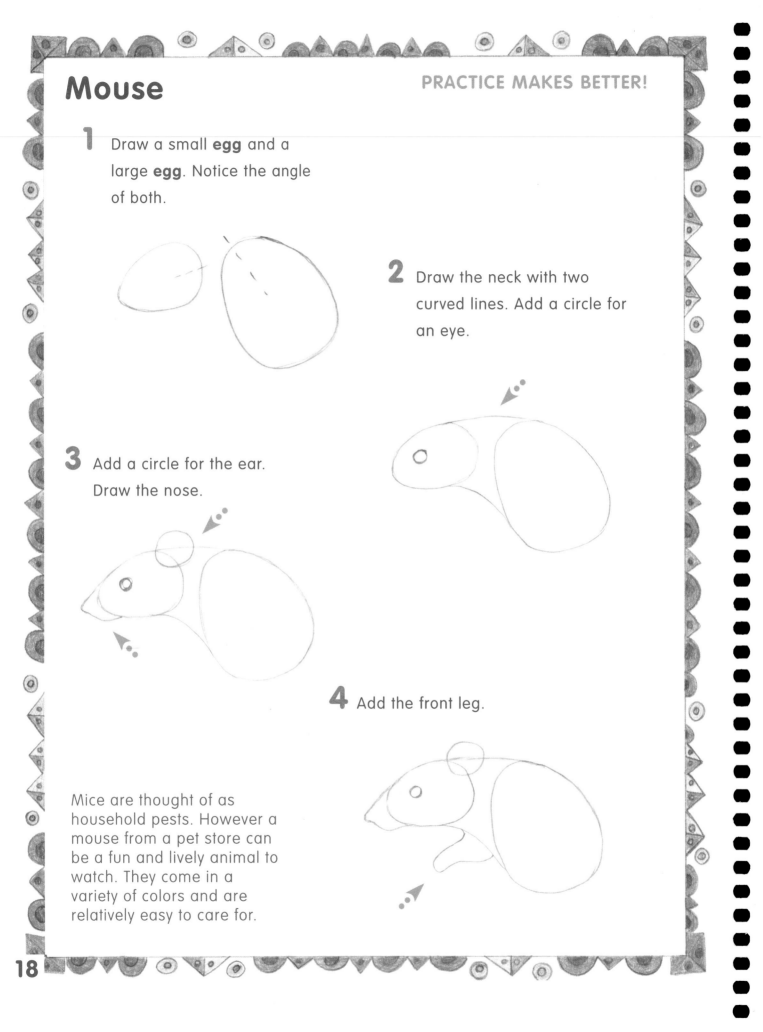

2 Draw the neck with two curved lines. Add a circle for an eye.

3 Add a circle for the ear. Draw the nose.

4 Add the front leg.

Mice are thought of as household pests. However a mouse from a pet store can be a fun and lively animal to watch. They come in a variety of colors and are relatively easy to care for.

5 Add a long thin tail. Add a hind leg.

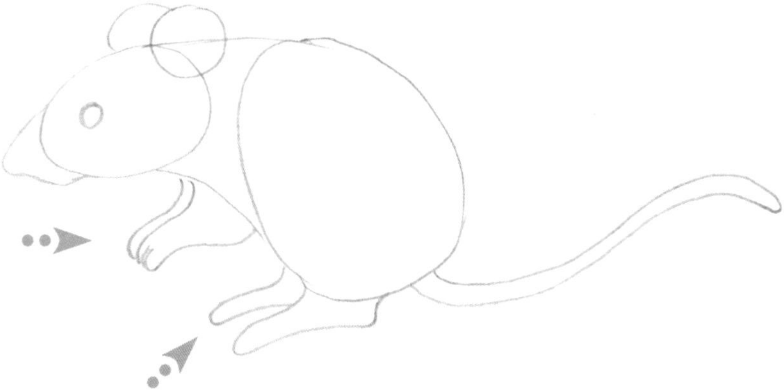

6 Draw the other ear. Make another front leg and hind leg.

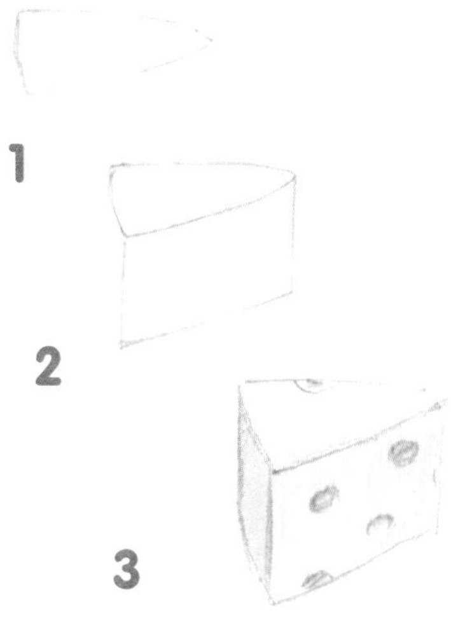

1

2

3

Make some cheese for your mouse!

7 Add some whiskers. Erase extra lines. Add shading. Darken the eye.

Gerbil

A gerbil is a rodent, a cousin to the mouse. Gerbils have fur on their tails. Their strong hind legs make them good leapers.

1 Start with an **egg** and a **circle**. Notice the angles.

2 Connect the egg and circle with curved lines. Make a dot for the eye.

3 Add two ears and a nose.

4 Draw a tail. Add a nose line. Draw three legs.

5 Erase extra lines. Use short pencil strokes to make your gerbil look furry.

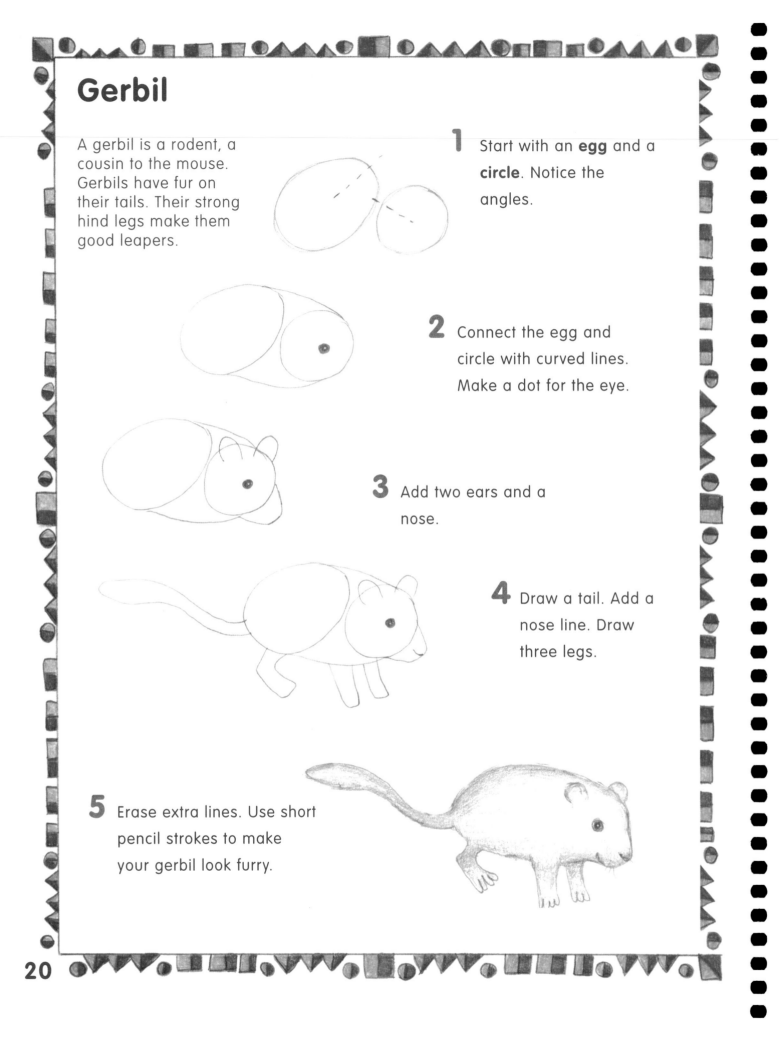

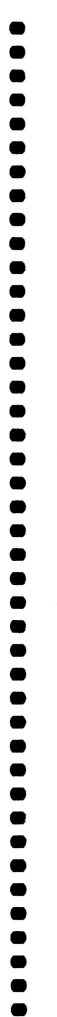

Guinea pig

1 Draw two **eggs**, one larger than the other. Notice how they **overlap**.

Guinea pigs are not pigs and they are not from Guinea. They are rodents, like mice and hamsters.

2 Make a dot for the eye. Add two curved lines to form the neck

3 Add two ears. Draw feet.

4 Add whiskers. Draw lines for markings.

5 Erase extra lines and add color to your creation!

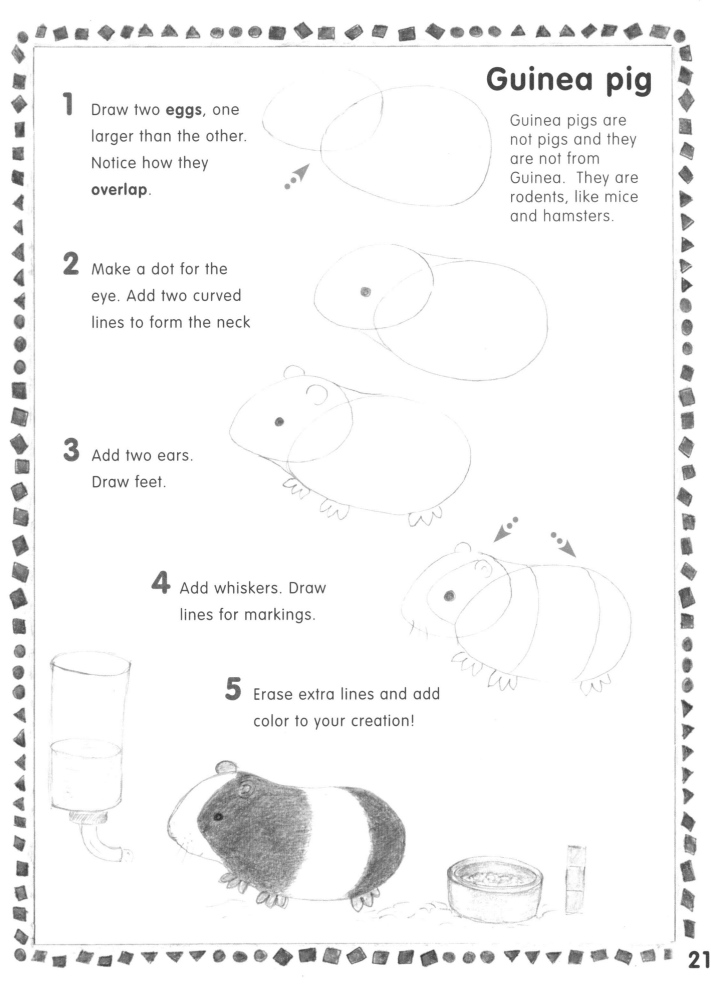

Hamster

Hamsters are nocturnal creatures. They are active at night.

1 Start with an **egg** and a **circle**. Notice the angle of the egg.

2 Draw a curved line connecting the egg and circle. Add a circle for the eye.

3 Draw two ears. Add the curve for the nose. Draw two hind feet.

4 Add another eye, nose and a front paw.

5 Make a second front paw. Add a stubby tail. Draw a line inside the ear.

6 Erase extra lines and add color and shading in the fur.

Happy hamster!

Rat

Some people dislike rats, but a purebred rat can make a lively and intelligent pet.

1 Draw a **circle** and an **egg**.

2 Draw curved lines for the neck and a circle for the eye. Add the nose.

3 Draw two ears. Draw the hind foot and a front leg.

4 Add a long skinny tail. The tail has no fur. Draw another front foot. Add the whiskers.

5 Erase extra lines and shade in fur and markings.

Iguana

1 Start with an **oval** and an **egg**.

2 Connect with curved lines, and draw the nose.

3 Add an eye bump, an eye, a nostril and a mouth.

4 Draw two legs.

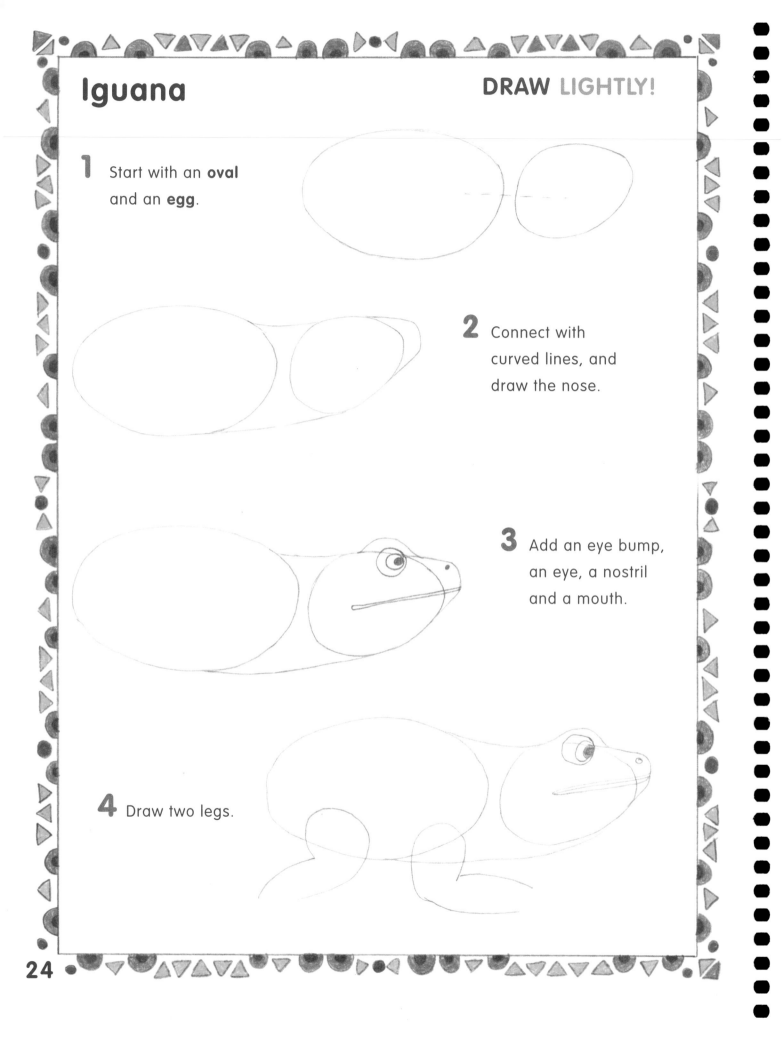

24

5 Add feet and claws.

6 Add a long curved tail. Draw bumpy scales on the back. Draw a wattle on the throat.

7 Erase extra lines. Color your iguana.

Iguanas can grow quite large.

It is best to get them when they are small and handle them daily to keep them tame.

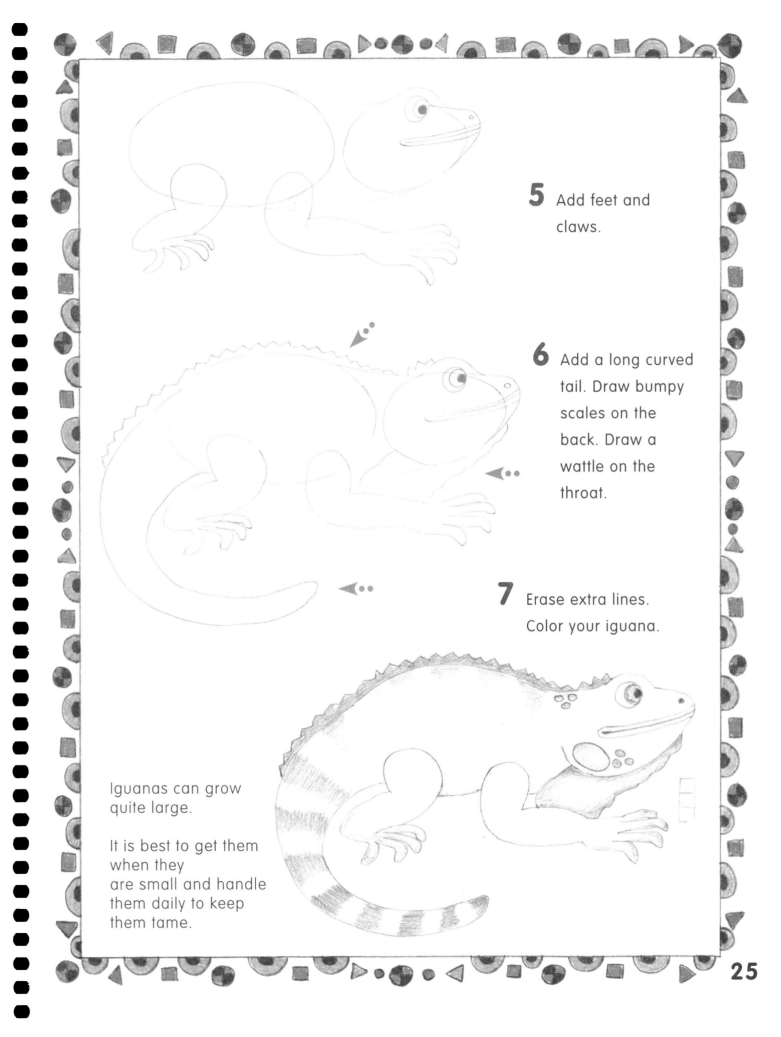

Gecko

1 Start with two small **ovals**. Notice how far apart they are.

2 Connect ovals with curved lines. Add an eye.

3 Add a curved tail. Draw a curve for the nose.

4 Add a line for the mouth, and a dot for the nose. Draw legs and feet.

5 Erase extra lines and color the markings. Give your gecko some rocks and plants. Great gecko!

Geckos' suction cup-like feet let them scurry up walls.

Chameleon

Chameleons can change color. This helps them blend in with their surroundings.

1 Start with an **oval** and a **circle**.

2 Add the crest shape. Draw the eye and mouth. Add a line for the throat.

3 Draw a spiral tail.

4 Draw scales on the back, and add the legs.

5 Erase lines and color your chameleon.

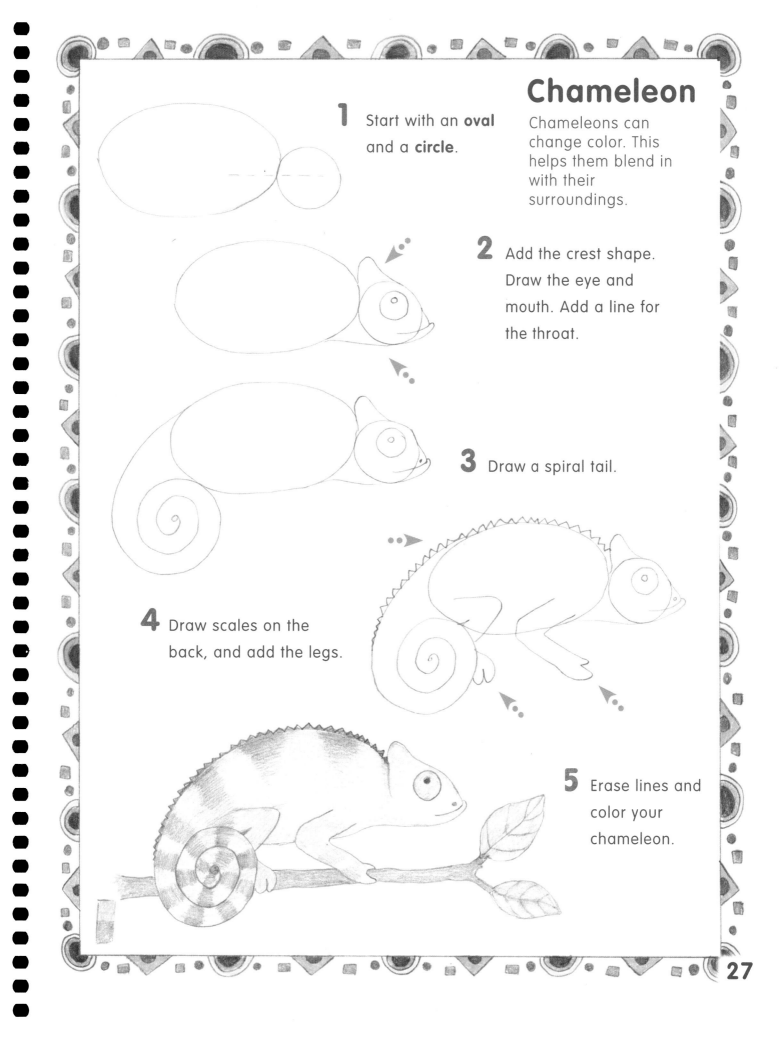

Turtle

1 Draw an **egg**.

2 Add lines on either end to make the shell shape.

3 Draw the head and neck.

4 Add an eye. Draw two legs.

5 Draw neck line, shell markings, and a tail. Add the lower shell called the plastron. Draw the toes.

6 Erase lines and add color.

Turtles have hard shells to protect them. Turtles have been on Earth since the time of the dinosaurs.

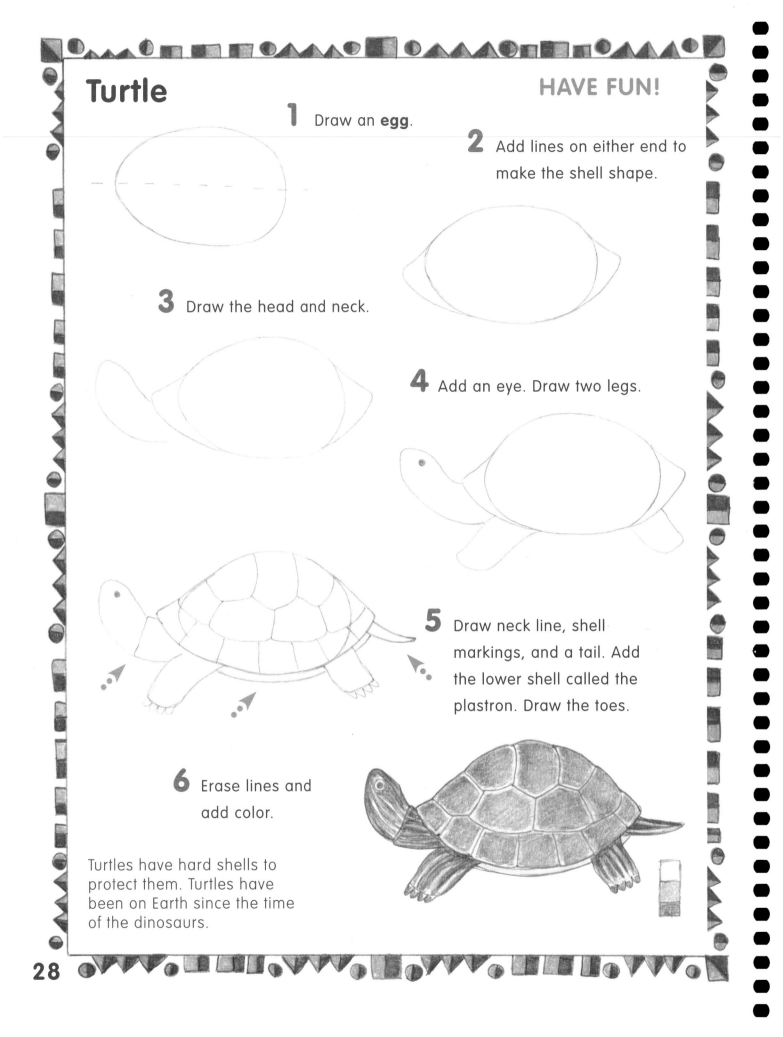

Frog

1 Draw two **eggs**, one larger than the other.

2 Draw a **circle** for the eye. Add another egg inside the large egg.

Frogs are amphibians. That means they can breathe in water and air.

3 Draw two neck lines, and a leg line.

4 Add a mouth. Draw feet and legs.

5 Add a bump for the other eye. Draw the eye and nose.

6 Erase lines and add color.

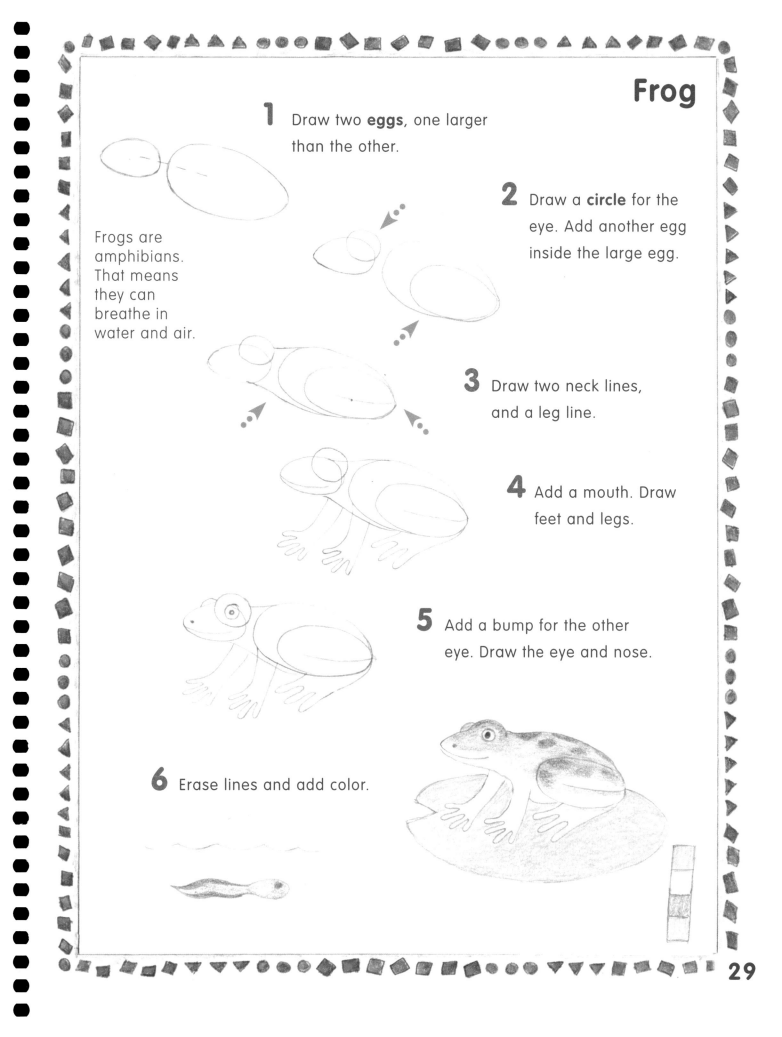

Goldfish

1 Start with an **oval**.

2 Add an eye and a
curve for the face.

3 Draw a **circle** around the eye.
Add a dorsal fin.

4 Draw a gill and add
three more fins.

5 Draw a fancy tail.

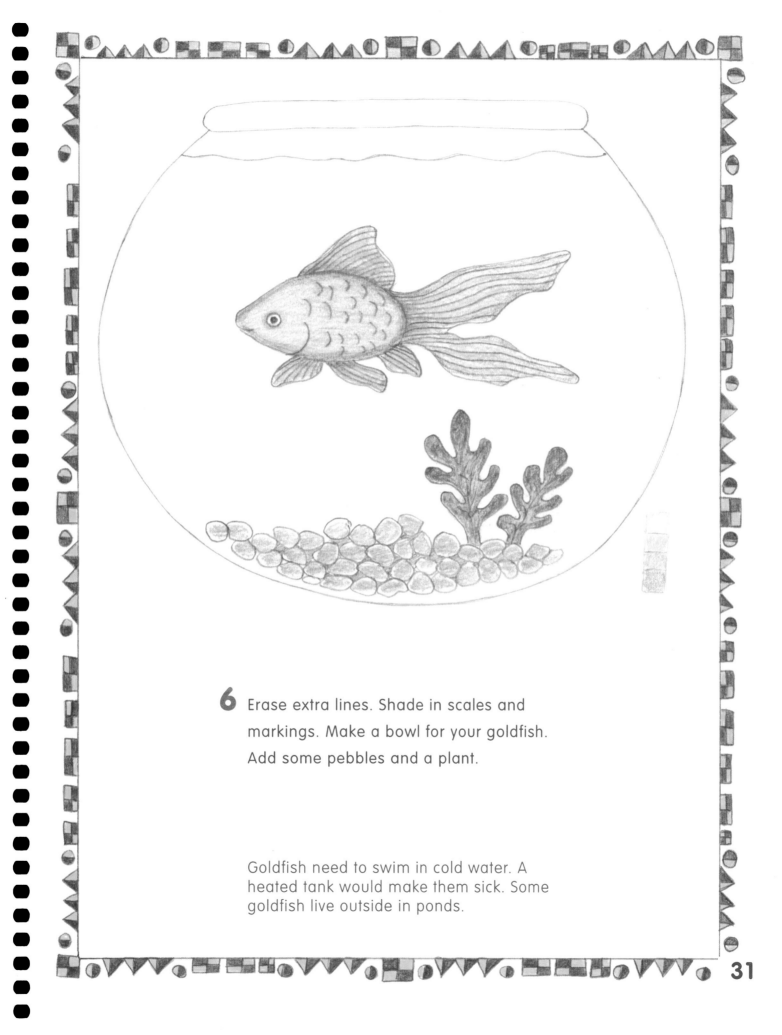

6 Erase extra lines. Shade in scales and markings. Make a bowl for your goldfish. Add some pebbles and a plant.

Goldfish need to swim in cold water. A heated tank would make them sick. Some goldfish live outside in ponds.

Aquarium fish
Angel fish

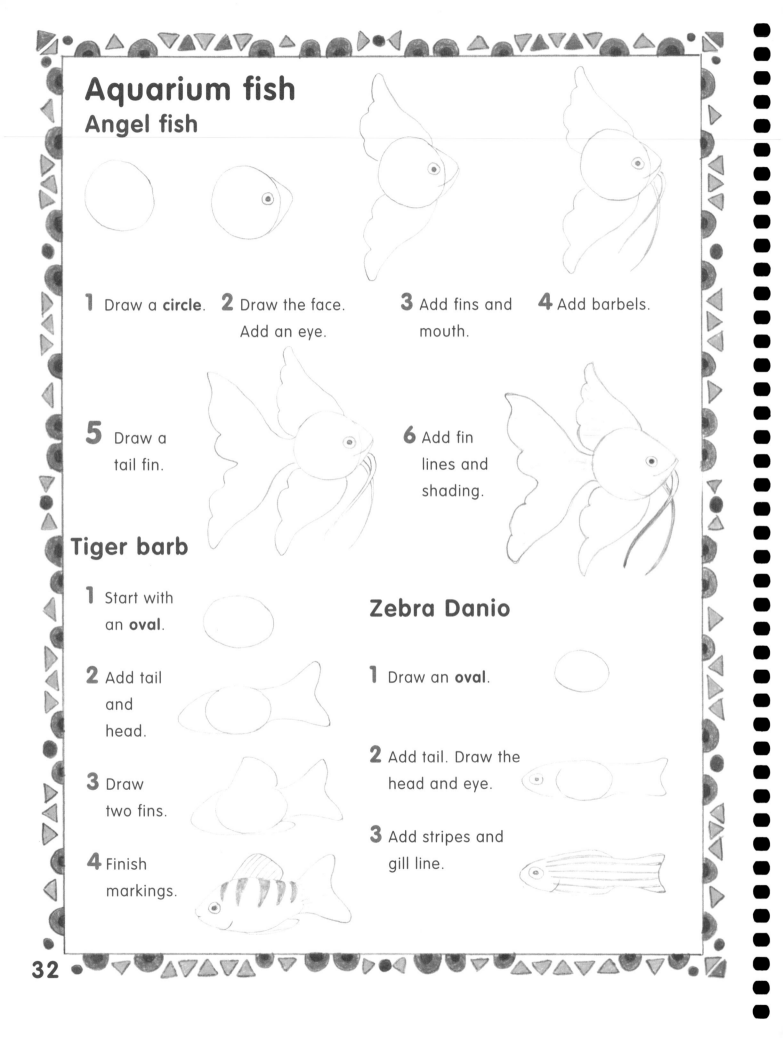

1 Draw a **circle**.

2 Draw the face. Add an eye.

3 Add fins and mouth.

4 Add barbels.

5 Draw a tail fin.

6 Add fin lines and shading.

Tiger barb

1 Start with an **oval**.

2 Add tail and head.

3 Draw two fins.

4 Finish markings.

Zebra Danio

1 Draw an **oval**.

2 Add tail. Draw the head and eye.

3 Add stripes and gill line.

Make an aquarium for your fish. Add rocks and plants.

Ferret

1 Draw three **eggs**. Notice how they are tipped and how far apart they are.

2 Connect the eggs with curved lines. Draw the tail. Make a circle for the eye.

3 Add legs and feet. Draw the ears.

Ferrets are in the weasel family. They have been kept as pets for thousands of years.

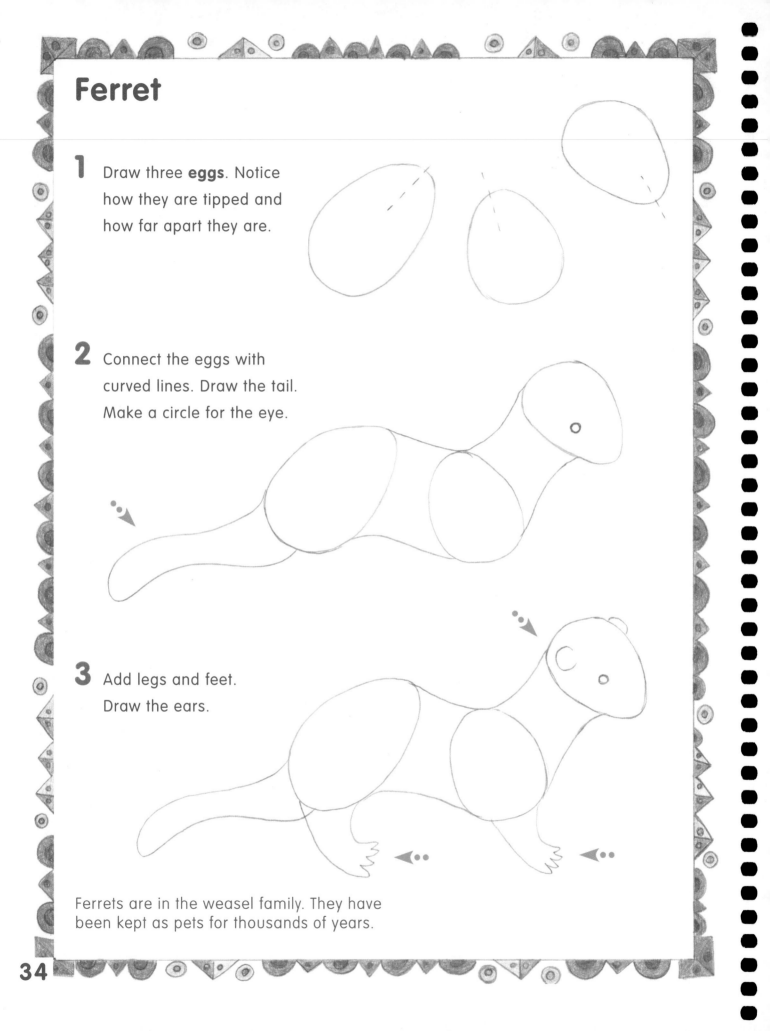

34

4 Add another eye and darken both eyes. Draw the nose and mouth. Add another foot.

5 Erase extra lines. Shade in markings. With short pencil strokes, draw fur. Draw the ferret's "bandit mask."

Fun ferret!

Make some toys for your playful ferret.

Tarantula

Not everybody might think a big, hairy spider would make a great pet.

However, they have become such popular terrarium animals that certain species have had to be protected in the wild lest they disappear.

1 Start with an **egg** and an **oval**.

2 Draw the start of four legs.

3 Start four more legs and draw six eyes.

4 Complete four legs. Add a mouth.

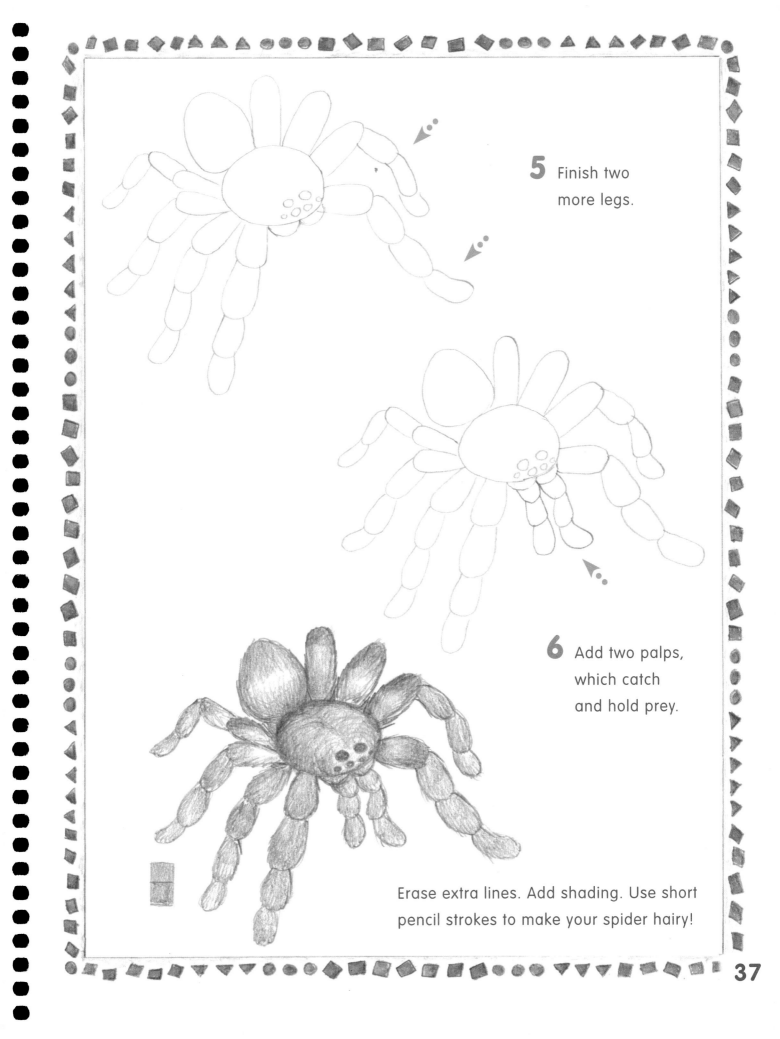

5 Finish two
more legs.

6 Add two palps,
which catch
and hold prey.

Erase extra lines. Add shading. Use short
pencil strokes to make your spider hairy!

Pigeon

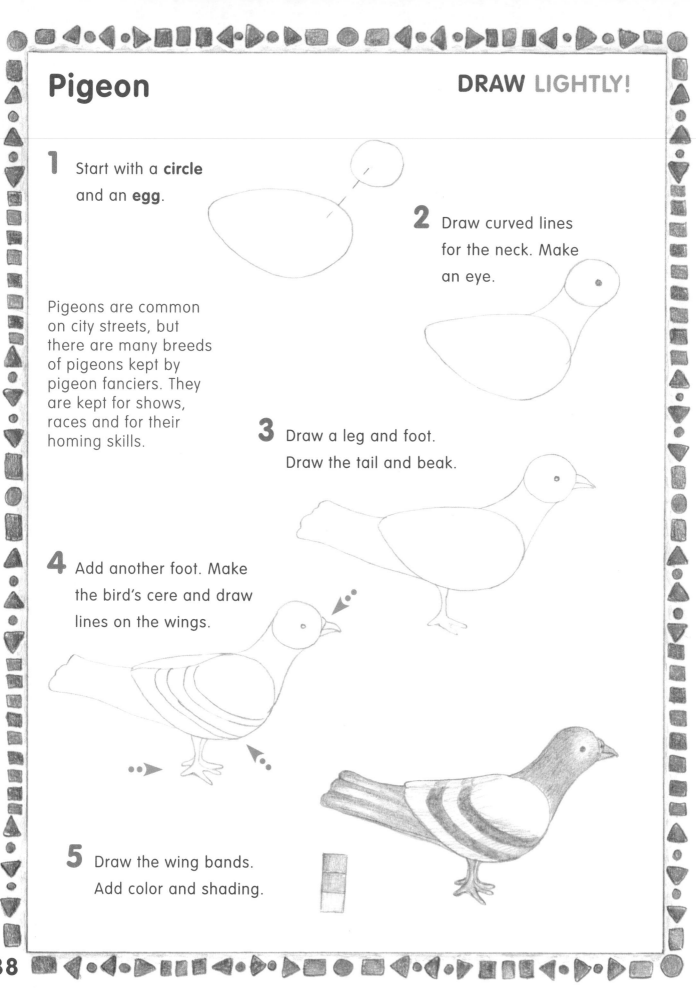

1 Start with a **circle** and an **egg**.

Pigeons are common on city streets, but there are many breeds of pigeons kept by pigeon fanciers. They are kept for shows, races and for their homing skills.

2 Draw curved lines for the neck. Make an eye.

3 Draw a leg and foot. Draw the tail and beak.

4 Add another foot. Make the bird's cere and draw lines on the wings.

5 Draw the wing bands. Add color and shading.

38

Pig

1 Start with a **circle** and an **oval**. Notice how they **overlap**.

2 Draw two legs. Add two eyes and the snout.

3 Draw the other two legs. Add two ears. Add two nostrils.

4 Erase extra lines. Draw a cuirly tail. Add shading. Color spots and hooves.

Pretty pig!

Add a curvy tail.

Pigs are smart animals. They can learn tricks like dogs. Pigs are not dirty animals, but roll in mud to protect their skin from sunburn.

Sheep

1 Start with an **oval** and a **circle**.

2 Add ears and an eye.

3 Draw the nose.
Draw two legs.

Sheep have warm, woolly coats. The wool is sheared in the spring. This does not hurt the sheep—it is like a haircut. The wool is spun into yarn and then made into warm hats, sweaters, mittens, and blankets.

40

4 Draw a little tail. Draw a line to form the face. Add two more legs.

5 Draw the inner ears. Add the neck. Draw hooves. Make your sheep woolly. Erase extra lines and add shading.

People have been herding sheep from before Biblical times.

Goat

1 Start with a big **egg** and a small **egg**.

2 Connect head and body with neck lines. Add two eyes.

3 Draw two legs. Add ears.

4 Add two more legs. Draw two horns.

5 Add a tail. Draw the inner ear lines. Draw a nose and mouth.

6 Add lines to horns. Make your goat shaggy. Draw hooves. Erase extra lines. Add shading.

Goats are cousins of sheep, but unlike sheep. do not have woolly coats. They are hardier than sheep and can adapt to many different types of environments.

Cow

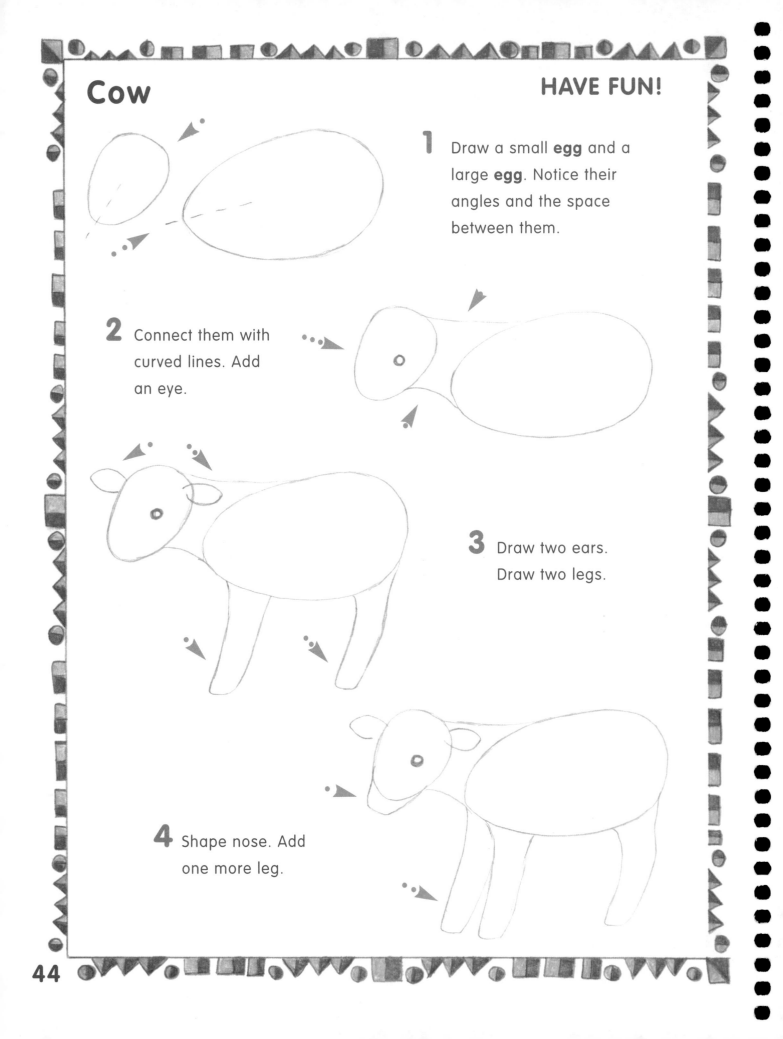

1 Draw a small **egg** and a large **egg**. Notice their angles and the space between them.

2 Connect them with curved lines. Add an eye.

3 Draw two ears. Draw two legs.

4 Shape nose. Add one more leg.

5 Draw a tail. Add the udder.

6 Draw two horns. Add one more leg. Add hooves and the tip of the tail.

7 Add spots. Finish tail. Shade and color.

Cows are famous for giving milk. One cow can give as much as eighty glasses a day. Black and white spotted cows are called Holsteins.

Duck

Webbed feet and oily feathers help a duck be at home in the water.

1 Start with a **circle** and an **egg**.

2 Make curved neck lines. Add an eye.

3 Add a bill. Draw tail feathers. Draw a leg.

4 Draw the wing. Add a webbed foot.

5 Add a second leg and foot. Erase extra lines. Add shading. Draw a pond for your duck to swim in.

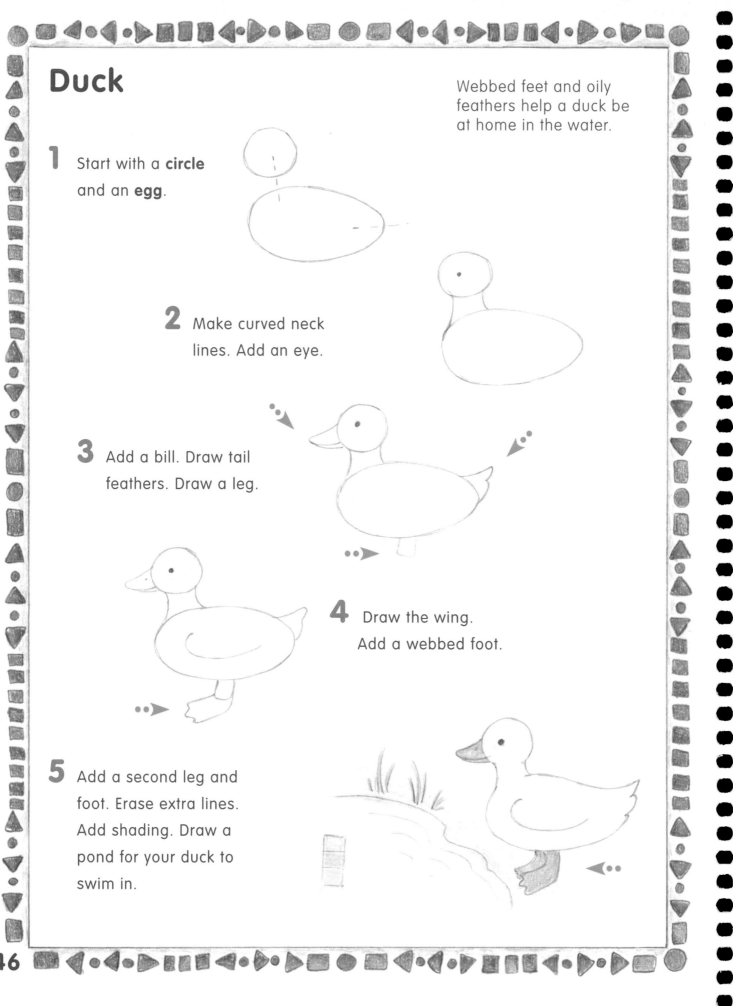

Goose

1 Draw a **circle** and an **egg**. Notice the distance between them.

2 Connect head and body with curving neck lines. Add an eye. Draw tail feathers.

3 Add the beak. Make a wing line. Draw two legs.

4 Draw webbed feet. Erase extra lines. Add shading.

A goose is taller than a duck and hardier than a chicken.

Rooster

1 Start with a big **egg** and a small **circle**.

2 Add an eye. Add curved neck lines.

3 Draw the rooster's comb and beak.

4 Add showy tail feathers. Draw wing line. Draw two legs.

5 Draw the rooster's wattle. Add feet.

6 Add neck feathers. Erase extra lines. Add shading and color.

1

2

Chick
Draw a baby chick.

3

Hen

1 Start with a big **egg** and a small **circle**. Notice the angles.

2 Add an eye. Add curved neck lines.

3 Draw a beak. Add a wing line. Draw tail feathers. They are smaller than the rooster's.

4 Make a small comb. Add two legs.

5 Add feet: three toes in front, one in back. Erase extra lines. Add shading and color.

Turkey

1 Start with a very small **circle** and a very big **egg**.

A baby turkey is called a poult. Turkeys have bumpy heads.

2 Add a beak. Draw the eye. Add one neck line. draw two legs.

3 Add feet: three toes in front and one in back.

4 Add the wattle. Add wing feathers.

5 Draw tail feathers. Erase extra lines. A shading and color.

Horse

1 Start with an **egg** and an **oval**. Notice the angles.

2 Add an eye. Add curved neck lines.

3 Draw the nose and add a nostril.

4 Add a front leg and a hind leg.

5 Add two more legs.

6 Add ears. Draw hooves and a tail.

Horses are no longer used for farming. They were replaced by trucks and tractors. They are kept now for riding, racing and rodeos.

On the next page are three ideas for dressing up your horse.

Put a saddle and bridle on your dapple gray.

Add a horn to make a unicorn.

Add wings to make a flying horse called Pegasus.

54

Donkey

1 Start with an **oval** and an **egg**. Notice the angles.

2 Add long ears. Add an eye. Draw neck lines.

3 Draw the start of a tail. Draw two legs.

Donkeys are horses' little cousins. They are sure-footed and still used in many places to carry burdens on rocky paths.

Donkey, continued

DRAW LIGHTLY!

4 Add a tail tuft. Add a nostril. Draw two more legs.

5 Draw a mane. Draw the inner ear lines. Lengthen the nose. Add hooves.

6 Erase extra lines. Add shading and color.

Bee

What a useful friend the bee is! A bee gives us honey and beeswax. It pollinates flowers and helps them grow. Farmers raise bees in apiaries.

1 Draw two **ovals**. Make them **overlap**. Notice the angles.

2 Draw two eyes.

3 Draw two wings.

4 Draw three legs.

5 Draw a proboscis. Add another leg.

6 Erase extra lines. Add stripes and shading.

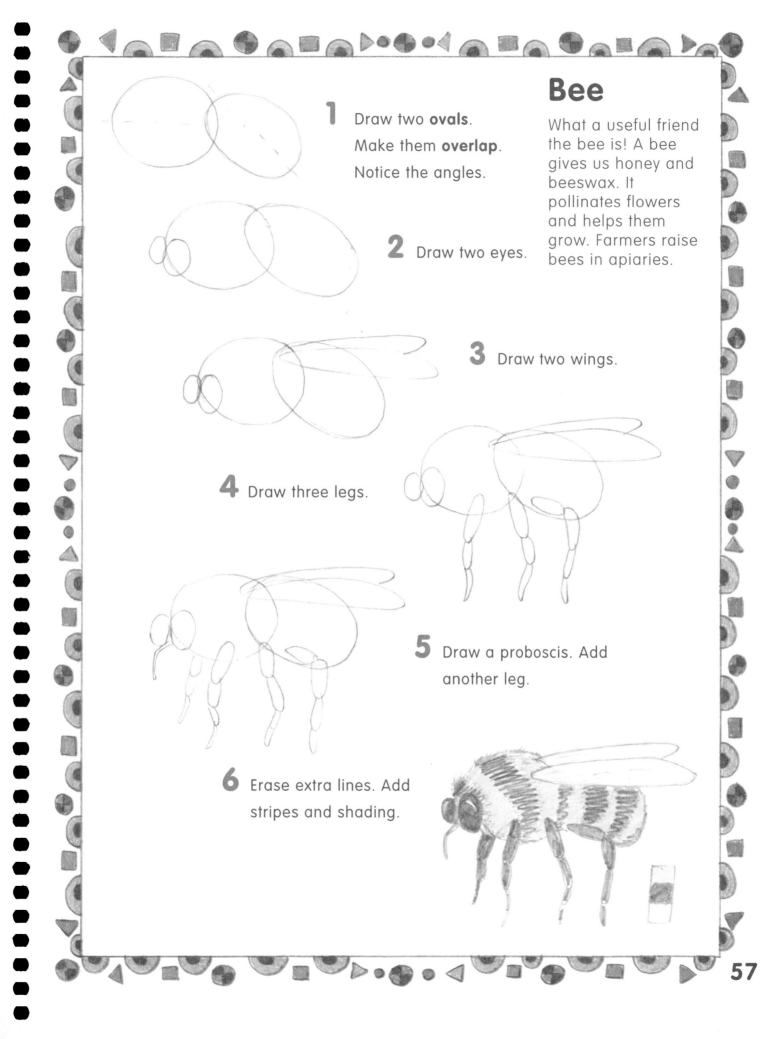

Squirrel

1 Start with three **ovals**: medium, small and large. Notice the angles.

2 Draw two ears. Draw the eye. Draw a curved line connecting neck and back.

3 Add the nose. Draw two curved lines to shape the tummy and the other back leg.

4 Add a line to the nose. Make two front paws and a chest line. Draw a hind foot.

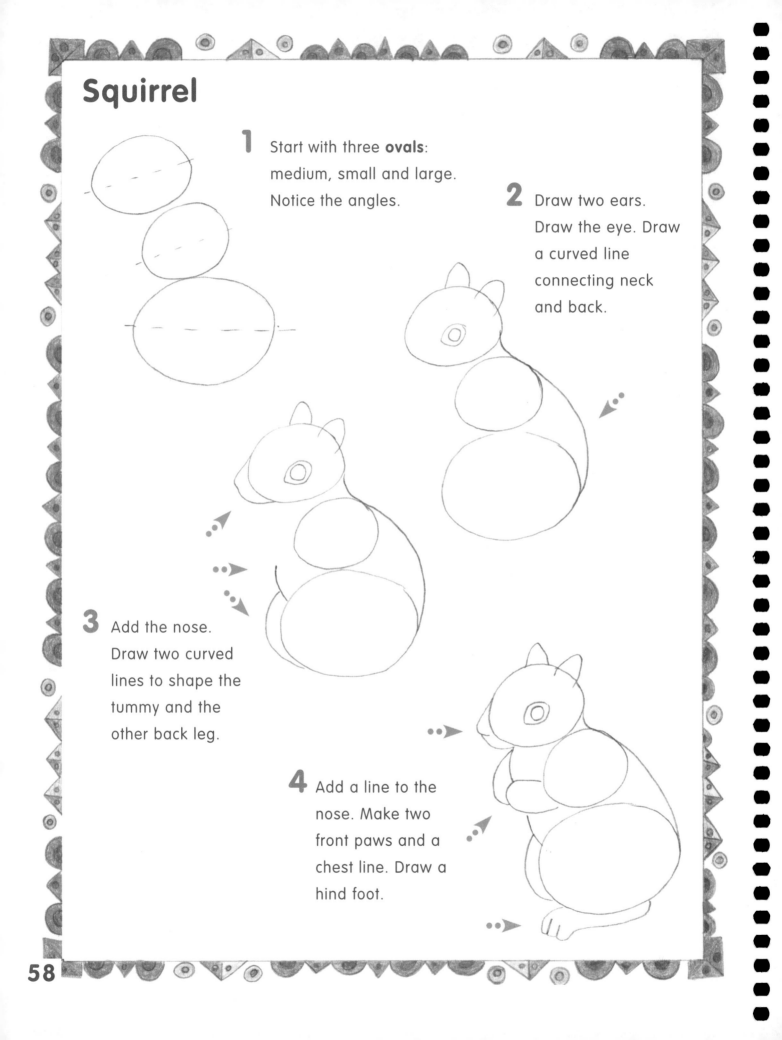

HAVE FUN!

5 Draw a big bushy tail. Add another hind foot.

6 Erase extra lines and shade markings. Make the tail furry.

Super squirrel!

Draw some acorns for your squirrel to bury.

Squirrels are in the rodent family. They are at home in the city or in the country. Always busy, they bury nuts and seeds for winter meals. They don't remember all of them and the forgotten food grows into new plants.

Crow

1 Start with a **circle** and an **egg**. Notice the angles.

2 Add an eye. Draw the neck.

3 Add a beak. Draw a wing.

4 Draw a tail and the tops of legs.

5 Add feather lines. Draw feet. Erase extra lines. Add shading and color.

A large, handsome bird, the crow is all black from head to toe.

Scarecrow

1 Start with a **square** and a **circle**. Make them **overlap**.

2 Add a face. Draw two **rectangles** for the arms.

3 Add two **rectangles** for trousers..

4 Add an **oval** for a hat brim. Draw two legs.

Farmers use scarecrows to keep birds from eating crops.

5 Draw the top of the hat. Add two buttons. Draw straw coming out of the sleeves.

6 Put patches on the trousers and a ragged edge. Erase lines. Add shading and color. Add a crow!

Butterfly

Butterfly wings are symmetrical. They are the same on both sides.

1 Draw the body.

2 Add wings.

3 Draw an inner line on each wing.

4 Add more wing markings.

5 Make tiny circles, like bubbles, in the wings' borders.

6 Fill black around the bubbles. Color and shade the markings.

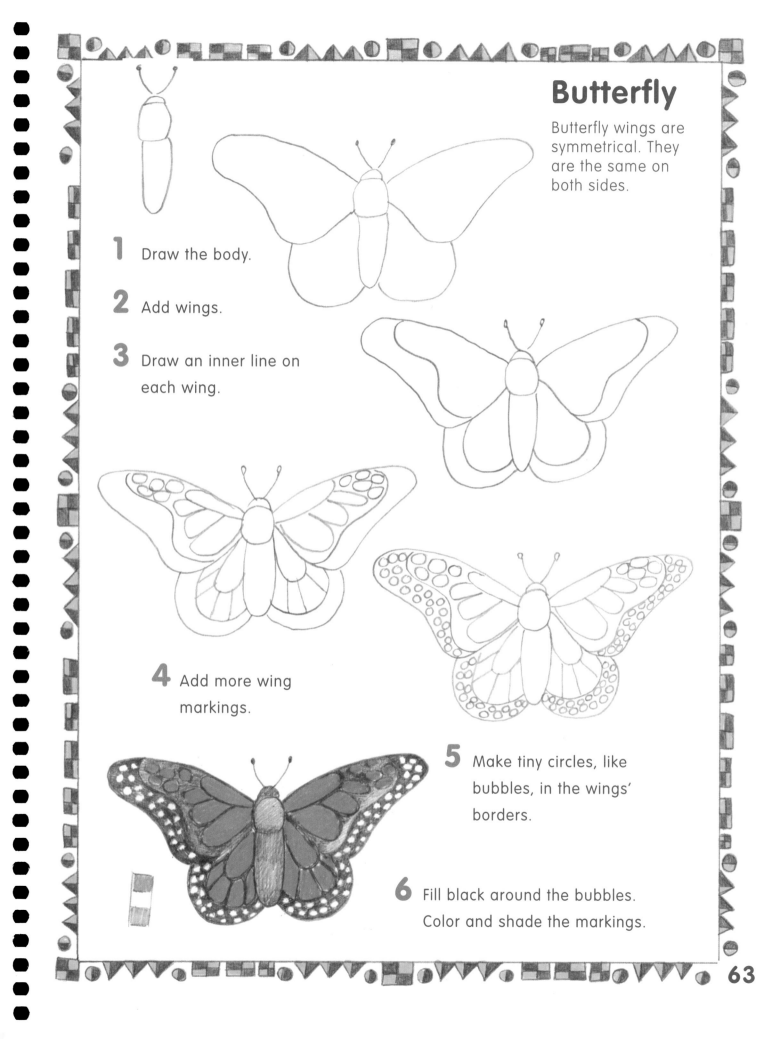

Index

Find more delectable
morsels online at
123draw.com!

1·2·3 Draw
DINOSAURS
and other Prehistoric Animals

A step
by step
guide

by
Freddie
Levin

Before you begin

You will need:

1. a pencil
2. an eraser
3. a pencil sharpener
4. lots of paper (recycle and re-use!)
5. colored pencils
6. a folder for saving work
7. a comfortable place to draw
8. good light

Now let's begin...!

Cataloging-in-Publication Data
Levin, Freddie.
  1-2-3 draw dinosaurs and other prehistoric animals /
  by Freddie Levin. p. cm.
  Includes index.
  ISBN 0-939217-41 -4 (pbk.)
  1. Dinosaurs in art--Juvenile literature. 2. Drawing--
Technique--Juvenile literature. I. Title: One-two-three
draw dinosaurs and other prehistoric animals. II. Title.

NC780.5 .L48 2000
743.6--dc21   00-057450

Distributed to the trade and art
markets in North America by

NORTH LIGHT BOOKS,
an imprint of F&W Publications, Inc.
4700 East Galbraith Road
Cincinnati, OH 45236

(800) 289-0963

Contents

Important drawing tip number 1:

*** Draw lightly at first, so you can erase extra lines. ***

Important drawing tip number 2:

*** Have fun drawing dinosaurs and other prehistoric animals! ***

Important drawing tip number 3:

*** Practice, practice, practice and you will get better! ***

Circles, Ovals and Eggs

The drawings in this book start with three basic shapes:

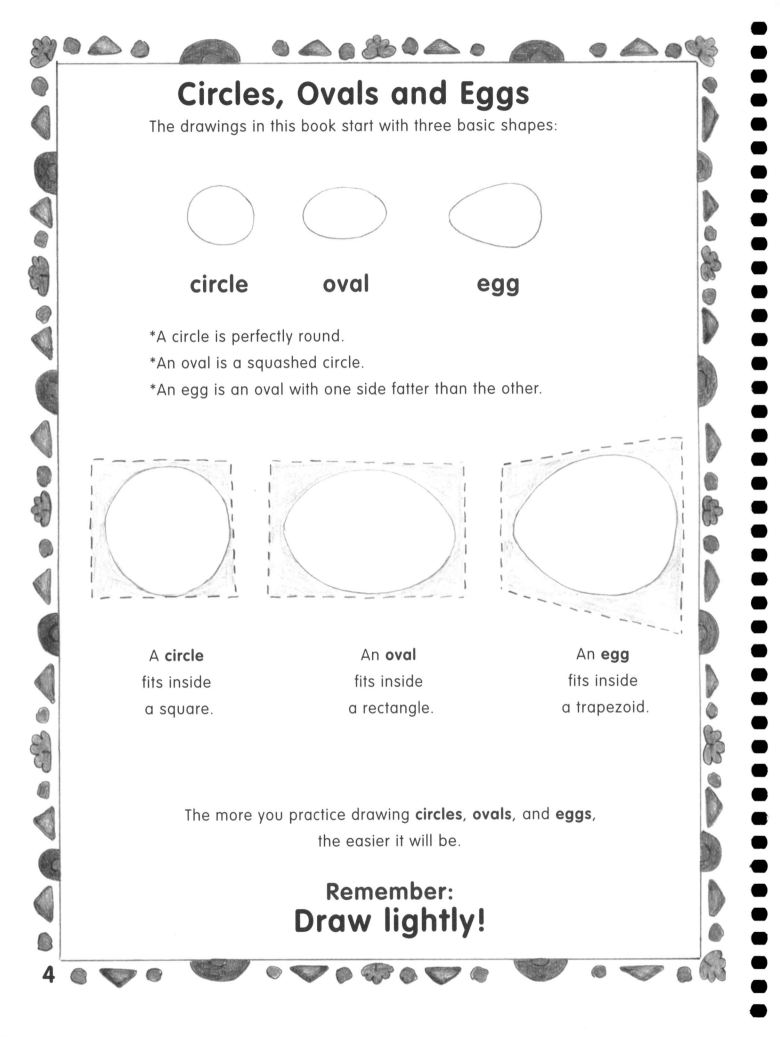

circle   **oval**   **egg**

*A circle is perfectly round.
*An oval is a squashed circle.
*An egg is an oval with one side fatter than the other.

A **circle**
fits inside
a square.

An **oval**
fits inside
a rectangle.

An **egg**
fits inside
a trapezoid.

The more you practice drawing **circles**, **ovals**, and **eggs**,
the easier it will be.

Remember:
Draw lightly!

What Color Were the Dinosaurs?

All the animals in this book are extinct. That means they died out long ago. Now we know them only from their bones. People who study these fossil bones are called paleontologists. Paleontologists can tell the appearance of dinosaurs and other animals by the shape of their bones.

We can only guess at their colors and markings. After all, who would know about a zebra's spectacular stripes from looking just at its bones? The reptile, bird and animal worlds have many colorful members.

So, have fun. Make your dinosaurs any color you want. I did!

Deinonychus

(dye - NON - ik - us)

Deinonychus means "terrible claw." It was small (11 feet long) and fast, and had good eyesight. It was named for the gigantic claw on its rear foot. Deinonychus hunted in packs. Its favorite food was meat.

1 Start with two **eggs**, one larger than the other.

2 Draw the neck. Shape the face. Draw a long pointy tail.

3 Add an eye and nose. Draw the mouth. Draw two front legs and feet. Draw back legs in sections. Add feet.

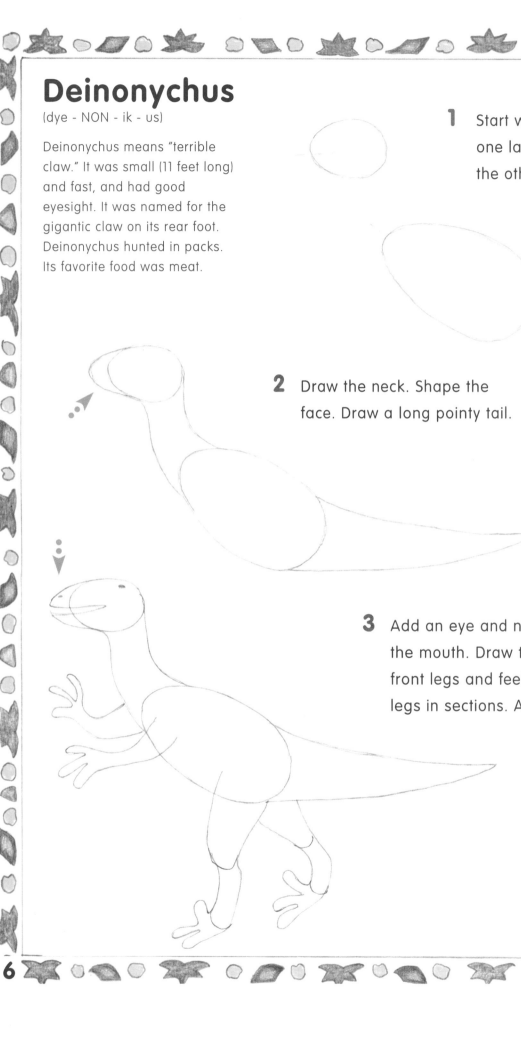

6

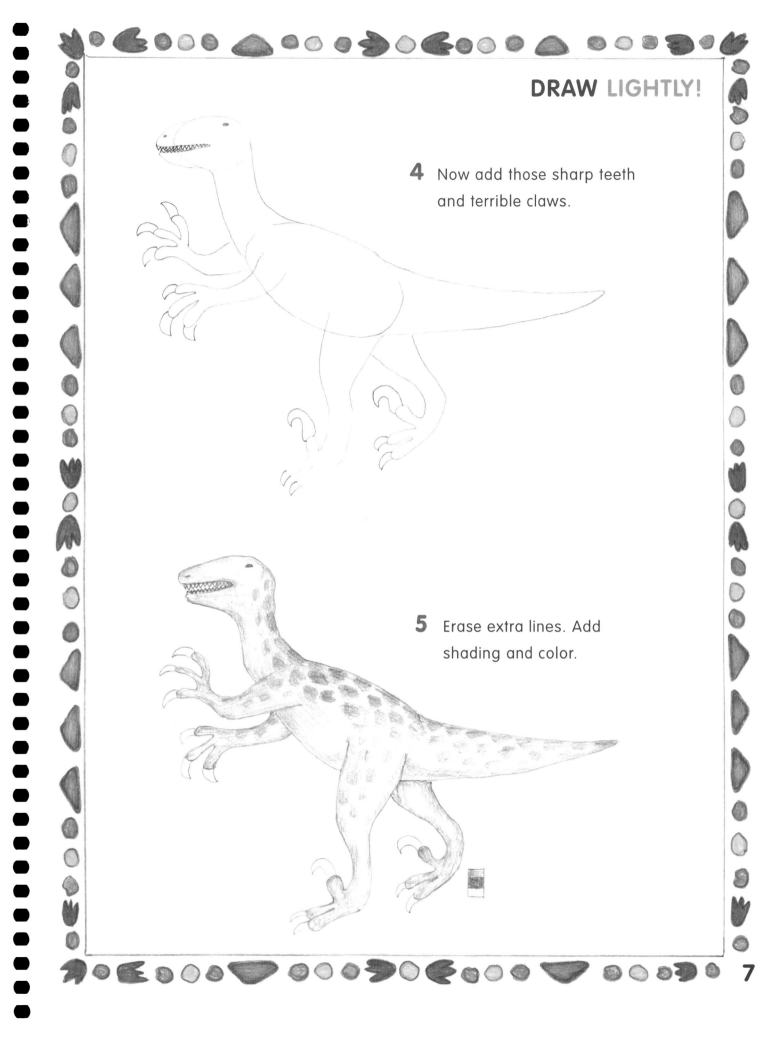

DRAW LIGHTLY!

4 Now add those sharp teeth and terrible claws.

5 Erase extra lines. Add shading and color.

Iguanodon

(ee - GWAN - oh - don)

Iguanodon means "iguana tooth." One of the first fossils ever found, it was thought the tooth looked like that of the modern iguana. Big as an elephant and equipped with thumb spikes, Iguanodon was a forest-dwelling plant eater.

1 Start with a **circle** and an **egg**.

2 Shape the face. Make a line for the mouth. Add a curved neck. Draw the tail.

3 Add an eye and a nostril. Draw a front leg and rear leg.

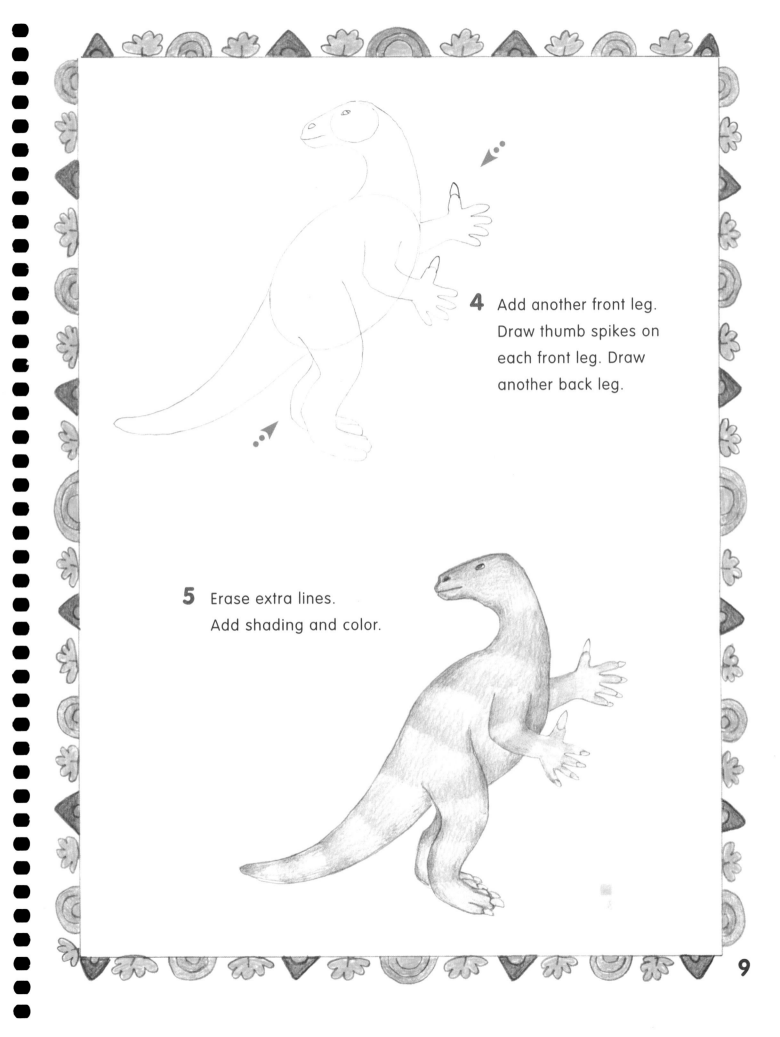

4 Add another front leg. Draw thumb spikes on each front leg. Draw another back leg.

5 Erase extra lines. Add shading and color.

Stegosaurus

(STEG - oh - SORE - us)

Tiny-brained Stegosaurus was 25 feet long, 11 1/2 feet high and weighed 2 tons. A plant eater, the bony plates and tail spikes were probably for protection.

1 Start with a large **oval** and a small **oval**. Notice the angle of the ovals.

2 Draw a curving tail. Shape the face and add an eye and nostril.

3 Add the bony plates all along the back. Notice that the ones in the middle are bigger. Draw two legs and feet.

10

4 Draw tail spikes. Add toenails.

5 Erase extra lines. Add shading and color.

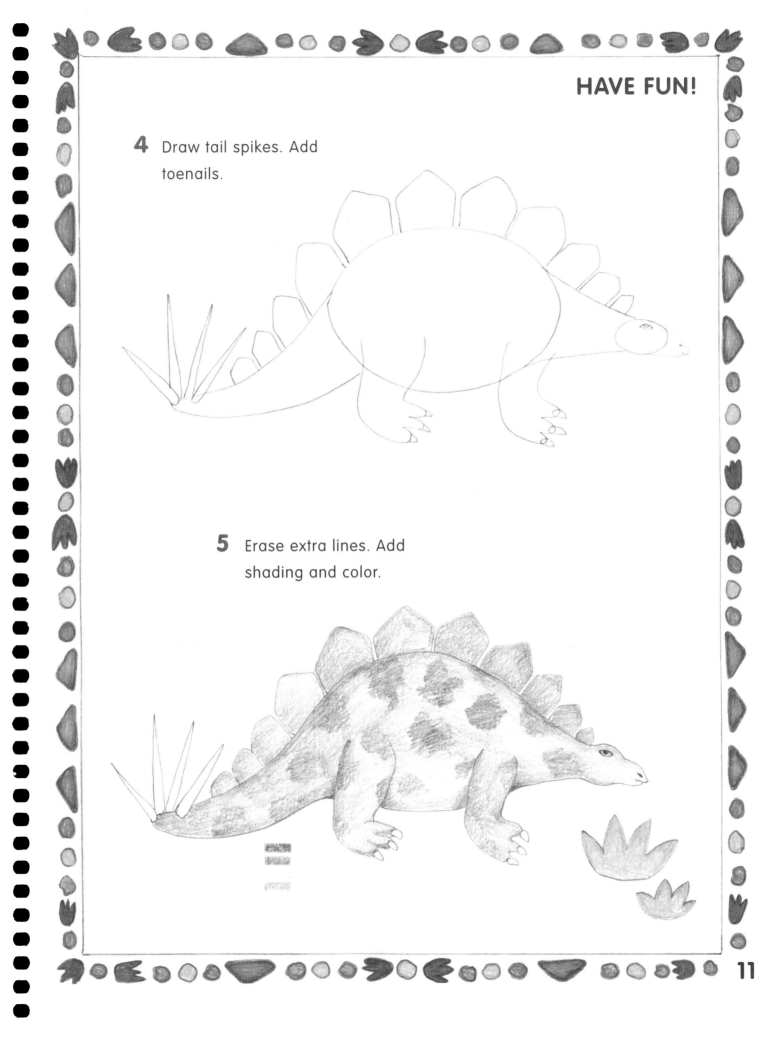

Tyrannosaurus

(ty - RAN - oh -SORE -us)

One of the best-known dinosaurs, this meat-eating terror had 6" long razor-sharp teeth and stood 40 feet tall. Some scientists believe that Tyrannosaurus was not a hunter but a scavenger who ate prey already dead.

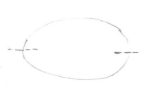

1 Start with a medium-sized **egg** and a large **oval**.

2 Add a mouth, nostril, and eye. Draw a curved neck. Add two front limbs. Draw four "U" shapes for the back legs.

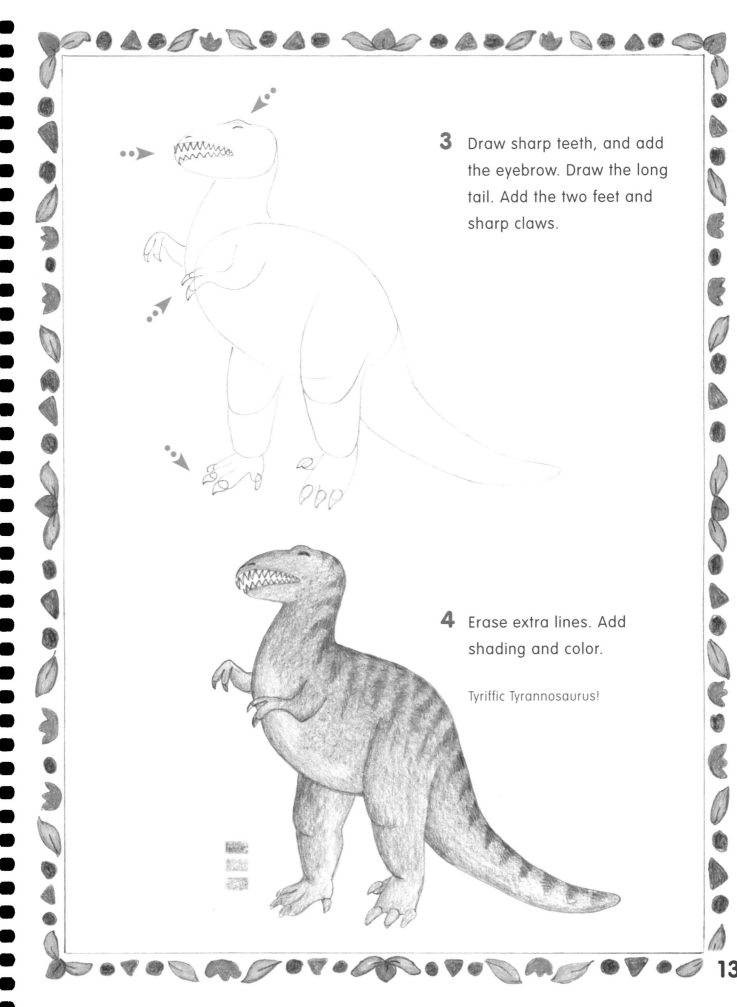

3 Draw sharp teeth, and add the eyebrow. Draw the long tail. Add the two feet and sharp claws.

4 Erase extra lines. Add shading and color.

Tyriffic Tyrannosaurus!

13

Ankylosaurus

(an - KY - low - sore - us)

Ankylosaurus means "stiff lizard."
It had bony plates and tail spikes
for protection. Ankylosaurus was a
plant eater.

1 Start with a small **circle**
and a big **egg**.

2 Add a beaklike mouth.
Draw the neck.

3 Draw the tail.

4 Shape the head. Add an
eye and a nostril. Draw a
tail knob.

5 Draw two legs and feet. Make knobs along the back. Draw a line through the middle of the body.

6 Draw a vertical line between each knob.

7 Draw rows of bumps, using the vertical lines as a guide. Add another front leg. Draw spikes on the tail.

8 Erase extra lines. Add detail lines and color.

Gallimimus

(Gal - i -MIME - us)

Gallimimus means "like a chicken." Its toothless beak and three-toed feet were bird-like, but it had arms instead of wings. Gallimimus was 17 feet tall, a fast runner and a plant eater.

1 Start with a small **circle** and a big **egg**.

2 Draw a curved, pointy beak and the eye. Draw the neck. Add a long pointy tail.

3 Draw an arm. Draw a leg, in two sections. Add a foot.

16

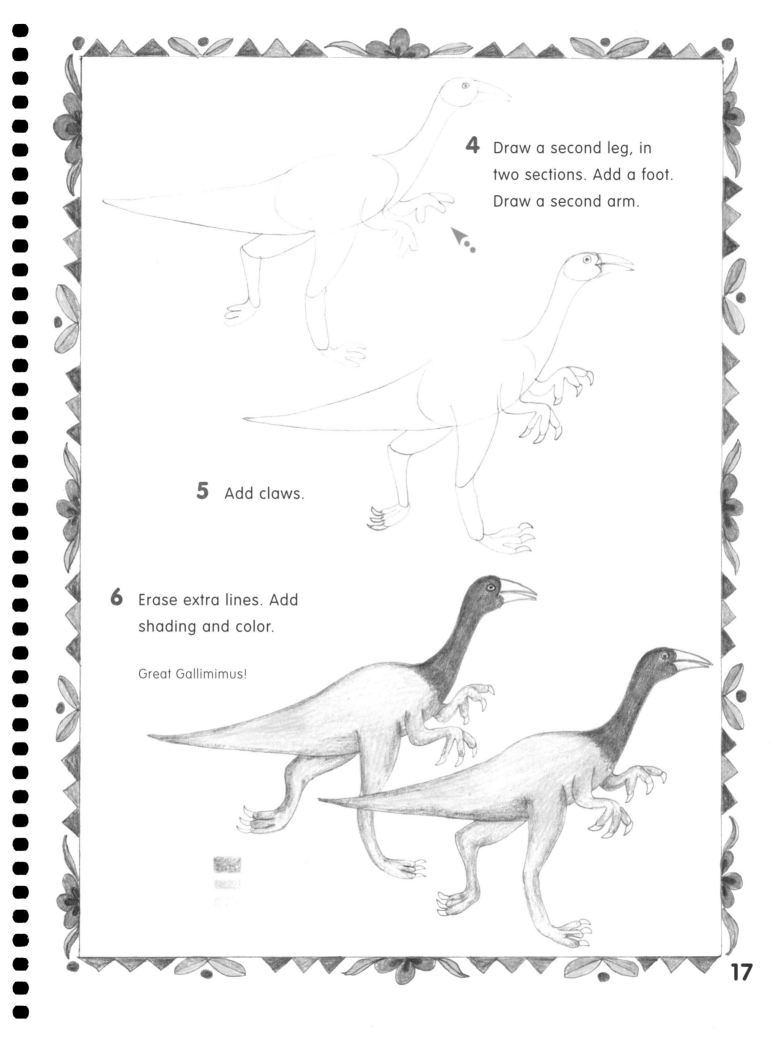

4 Draw a second leg, in two sections. Add a foot. Draw a second arm.

5 Add claws.

6 Erase extra lines. Add shading and color.

Great Gallimimus!

Diplodocus

(Dih - PLOD - uh - kuss)

Diplodocus means "double beam," which refers to the shape of its backbone. Diplodocus was a 90-foot-long plant eater. It had nostrils on top of its head so that it could be almost totally submerged in water.

1 Start with a tiny **egg** and a big **oval**.

2 Draw a long curved neck. Shape the face and add an eye.

3 Add two legs.

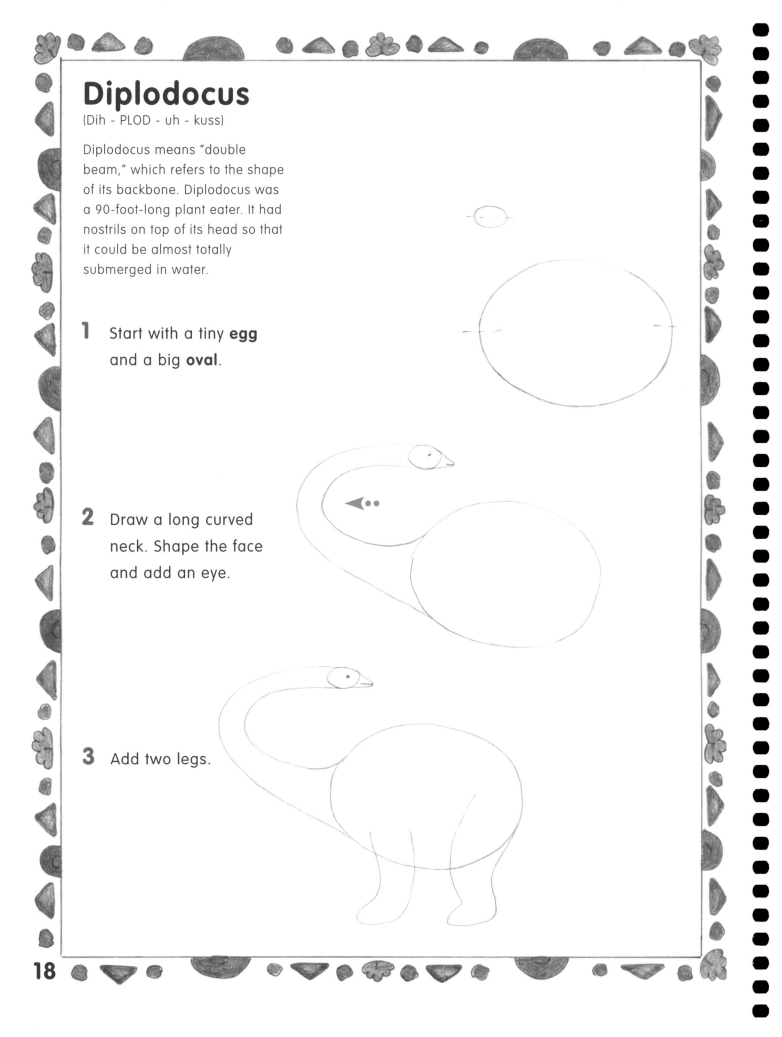

4 Add two more legs. Draw a long, snakelike tail.

5 Erase extra lines. Add shading and color.

Delightful Diplodocus!

Parasaurolophus

(par - ah - sore - OL - uh - fuss)

Parasaurolophus was a member of the duck-billed dinosaur family. Lambeosaurus was its cousin (see page 36). The tube on its head was hollow and connected to its nostrils. It is believed that Parasaurolophus could make loud bellowing noises through its horn. It was a forest dweller who ate mostly leaves, seeds, and twigs.

1 Start with a **circle** and an **oval**.

2 Draw the face. Add an eye. Draw the neck lines. Add a front leg. Draw a rear leg.

3 Add a horn. Make a circle around the eye. Add the nostrils. Add another front and back leg.

Some Parasaurolophus had horns that were six feet long!

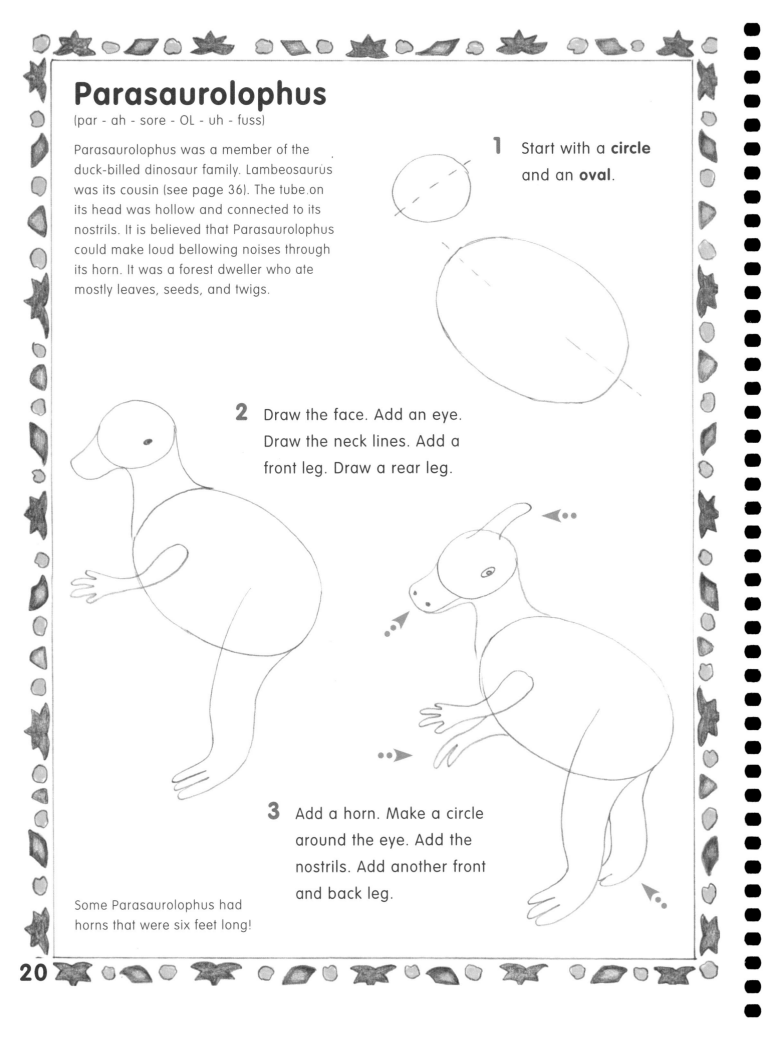

4 Add claws.

5 Erase extra lines. Add shading and color.

21

Pachycephalosaurus

(pake - ee - sef - uh - lo -SORE - us)

Pachycephalosaurus was a "bone-head" dinosaur. The top of its skull was twenty times thicker than a person's. It was a lot like having a bowling ball on your head. It may have been used in rivalries or to butt enemies. Pachycephalosaurus, 15 feet tall, had a very hard head and a very small brain.

1   Start with two **eggs**. Notice the angles.

2   Add an eye. Draw a curved neck.

3   Add a front leg and a back leg in three sections.

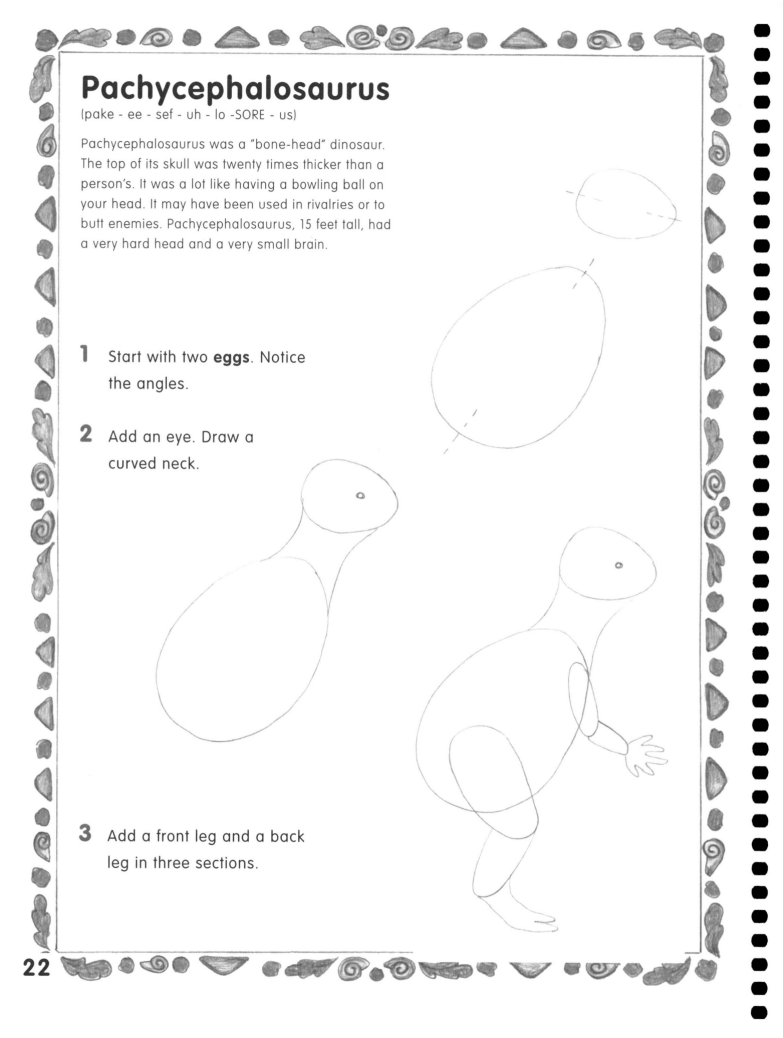

22

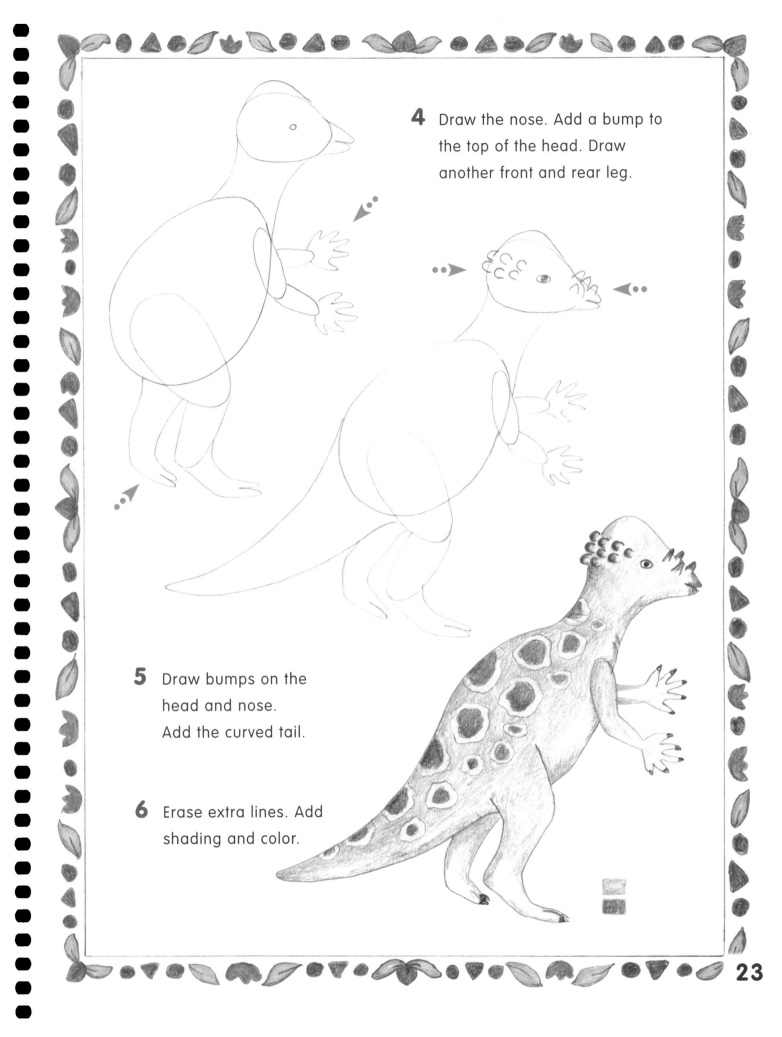

4 Draw the nose. Add a bump to the top of the head. Draw another front and rear leg.

5 Draw bumps on the head and nose. Add the curved tail.

6 Erase extra lines. Add shading and color.

Psittacosaurus

(sih - TAK - ah - SORE - us)

Psittacosaurus means "like a parrot," because it had a jaw shaped like a beak. It was a cousin to Triceratops (see page 35). Only five feet tall, Psittacosaurus was a plant eater that walked on all fours.

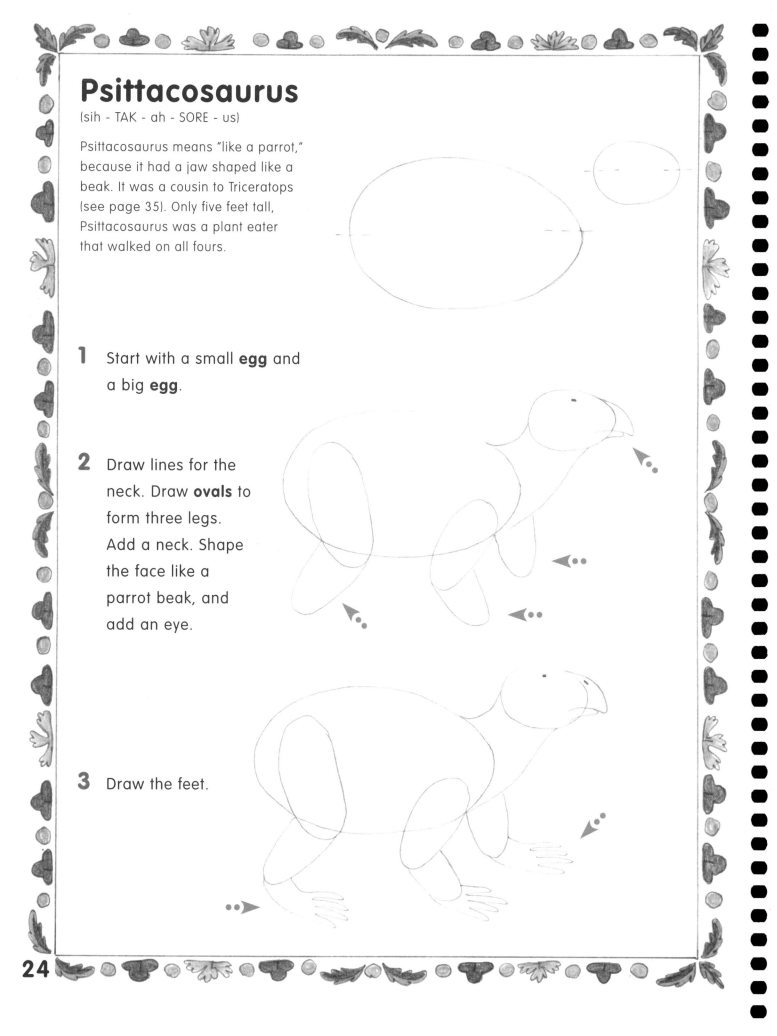

1 Start with a small **egg** and a big **egg**.

2 Draw lines for the neck. Draw **ovals** to form three legs. Add a neck. Shape the face like a parrot beak, and add an eye.

3 Draw the feet.

4 Draw a curving tail.

5 Erase extra lines. Add shading and color.

Pretty Psittacosaurus!

Velociraptor

(Vuh - LOSS - ih - RAP - tor)

Velociraptor means "speedy thief." Only 6 feet tall, this meat eater had sharp eyesight. Velociraptor may have hunted in dim light or at night.

1 Start with an **egg** and a long **oval**.

2 Draw the neck. Shape the face and jaw. Add an eye and nostril. Draw the shapes of the front and back legs.

3 Add claws. Erase extra lines. Add shading and color.

26

Pteranodon

(ter - AN - o -don)

Pteranodon means "winged and toothless" and was more of a glider than a flier. It was the size of a turkey and ate fish.

1 Start with an **oval** and an **egg**. Notice the angles.

2 Draw the neck, head and beak. Add the eye.

3 Draw two "arms" with extra long finger bones. Add two legs.

4 Attach wings to finger bones. Erase extra lines. Shade and color.

27

Archaeopteryx

(ar - kay - OP - ter - icks)

Archaeopteryx means "ancient wings." One of the first birds, it was the size of a crow. It had feathers and bones like a bird, but it also had claws, teeth, and a long bony tail like a dinosaur.

1 Start with a **circle** and an **egg**.

2 Draw the neck. Draw an eye and a beak. Looking carefully at the example, draw two wings. Add a long tail.

3 Draw lines in wings and widen the tail. Add claws to the wings. Draw teeth. Draw legs and feet.

5 Draw feathers on the wings. Use the curved line you drew to guide you in drawing the feather pattern. Add tail feathers.

6 Erase extra lines. Add shading and color.

Spinosaurus

(SPY - no - SORE - us)

Spinosaurus means "spiny lizard." The sail on its back could open like a fan and probably was used as a heat regulator. Meat-eating spinosaurus had teeth as sharp and serrated as steak knives.

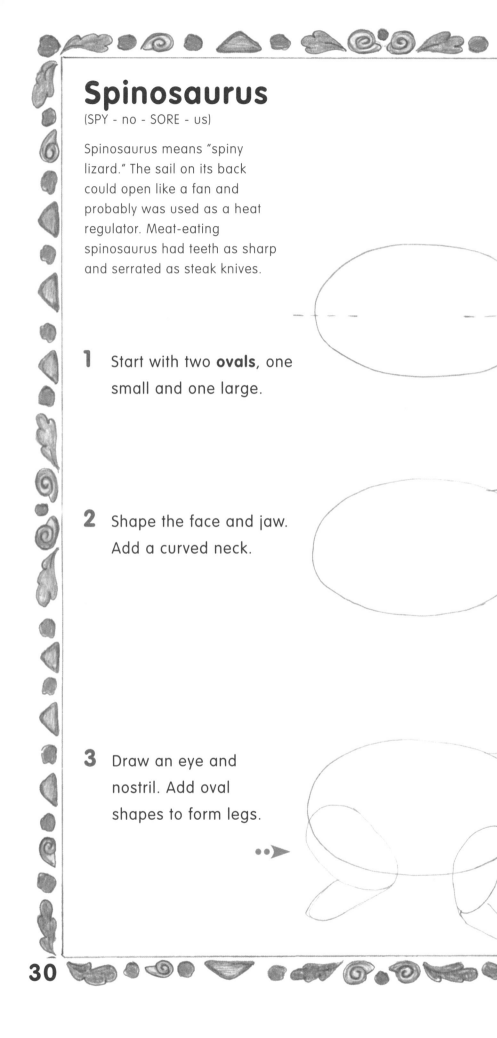

1 Start with two **ovals**, one small and one large.

2 Shape the face and jaw. Add a curved neck.

3 Draw an eye and nostril. Add oval shapes to form legs.

30

4 Finish the eye. Add teeth. Add the other back leg. Draw feet. Add the tail. Draw the back sail.

5 Add vertical lines to the back sail. Erase extra lines. Add shading and color.

Super Spinosaurus!

Ichthyosaurus

(ICK - thee - oh - SORE - us)

Ichthyosaurus was not a true dinosaur but a marine reptile. About 6 feet long and a good swimmer, Ichthyosaurus gave birth to live young.

1 Start with an **oval** and a **circle**. Draw the neck and head, and add an eye.

2 Draw the tail. Add a dorsal fin.

3 Add flippers and teeth.

4 Erase extra lines. Add shading and color.

Elasmosaurus

(ee - LAZ - mo - SORE - us)

Elasmosaurus was a swimming reptile. Its long snaky neck was as long as its body. Elasmosaurus had strong jaws and sharp teeth, and ate fish.

1 Start with a small **oval** and a big **oval**.

2 Connect ovals with two long snaky neck lines. Draw a pointy nose. Add an eye.

3 Add the mouth. Draw two flippers. Add two more flippers and a tail.

4 Erase extra lines, and add shading and color.

33

Compsognathus

(komp - so - NAY - thus)

Compsognathus means "pretty jaw." With hollow bones and birdlike feet, it was the size of a chicken. Fast and agile, compsognathus ate small mammals and lizards.

1 Start with a small **oval** and a larger **oval**. Notice how far apart they are.

2 Draw a beak, eye, and long curved neck.

3 Draw short front legs. Draw running legs in two sections. Add feet. Draw the long tail.

4 Erase extra lines. Add shading and color.

Triceratops
(try - SER - a - tops)

Triceratops means "three horns." A 30-foot-long, 6-ton plant eater, its horns were for protection and fighting its rivals.

1 Start with an **oval** and a **circle**.

2 Shape the head and add the beaklike mouth. Add an eye. Add a curved tail. Draw two legs.

3 Draw three horns. Add another back leg. Draw another front leg.

4 Erase extra lines. Add shading and color.

Terrific Triceratops!

Lambeosaurus

(LAM - bee - oh - SORE - us)

Lambeosaurus was named after Canadian fossil hunter Lawrence Lambe. It was a duck-billed dinosaur related to Parasaurolophus (see page 20). The bony crest had nostrils in it, and may have used to make sounds and for recognizing individuals. Lambeosaurus was 30 to 50 feet long.

1 Start with a small **egg** and a large **oval**.

2 Add the odd-shaped head bone. Shape the face and jaw. Add nostril and eye. Draw the curving neck.

3 Draw ovals to shape the two front legs and one back leg.

4 Draw front and back feet, with toe nails. Add a curving tail.

5 Erase extra lines. Add shading and color.

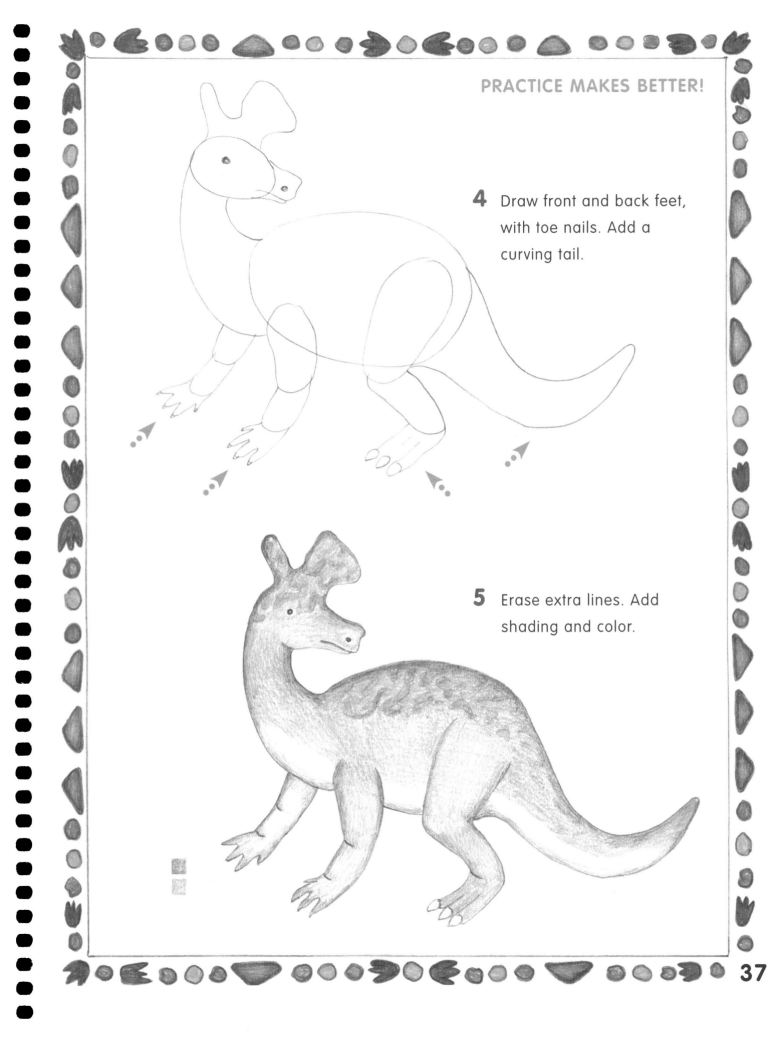

Kentrosaurus

(KEN - tro - SORE - us)

Kentrosaurus means "spiked lizard."
It was a cousin of Stegosaurus (see
page 10). Tiny brained and toothless,
Kentrosaurus was a plant eater that
walked on all fours. It probably lived
in herds and weighed up to 17 tons.

1 Start with a tiny **circle**
and a big **egg**.

2 Draw the neck by connecting the
two ovals. Shape the face and jaw.
Add a nostril, mouth and eye.

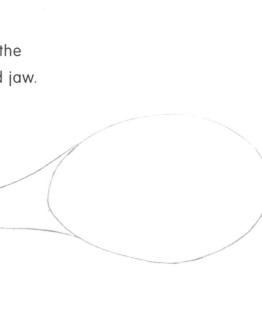

38

3 Draw ovals to make the front and back legs. Draw the tail. Add feet.

4 Draw back plates half way up the back, then draw spikes all the way to the tail.

5 Erase extra lines. Add shading and color.

Maiasaurus

(My - ah - SORE - us)

Maiasaurus means "good mother lizard." One of the duck-billed dinosaurs, it was about 30 feet long and a plant eater. At a Montana site, fossil hunters discovered an area that contained almost 40 nests, 6 feet across and dug out of the ground. Maiasaurus was indeed a good mother who nurtured her foot-long babies.

1 Start with a big **egg** and a small **egg**.

2 Draw a neck. Add a bump on the head. Shape the nose and jaw. Add an eye and nostril.

3 Draw ovals to make four legs.

4 Add four feet and claws. Draw a tail.

5 Erase extra lines. Add shading and color.

Marvelous Maiasaurus!

Morganucodon

(mor - guh - NUKE - uh - don)

Morganucodon was a tiny mammal that lived alongside dinosaurs. It survived by being active at night and eating insects, seeds, and eggs. After dinosaurs disappeared, around 65 million years ago, mammals like Morganucodon took over and began evolving in many different ways.

1 Draw a small **circle** and an **egg**.

2 Shape face and jaw. Draw the neck. Make a circle for the back leg. Draw the front leg and paw. Make a dot for the eye.

3 Add whiskers. Draw an ear. Add another front leg. Draw a long tail.

4 Erase extra lines. Add shading and color.

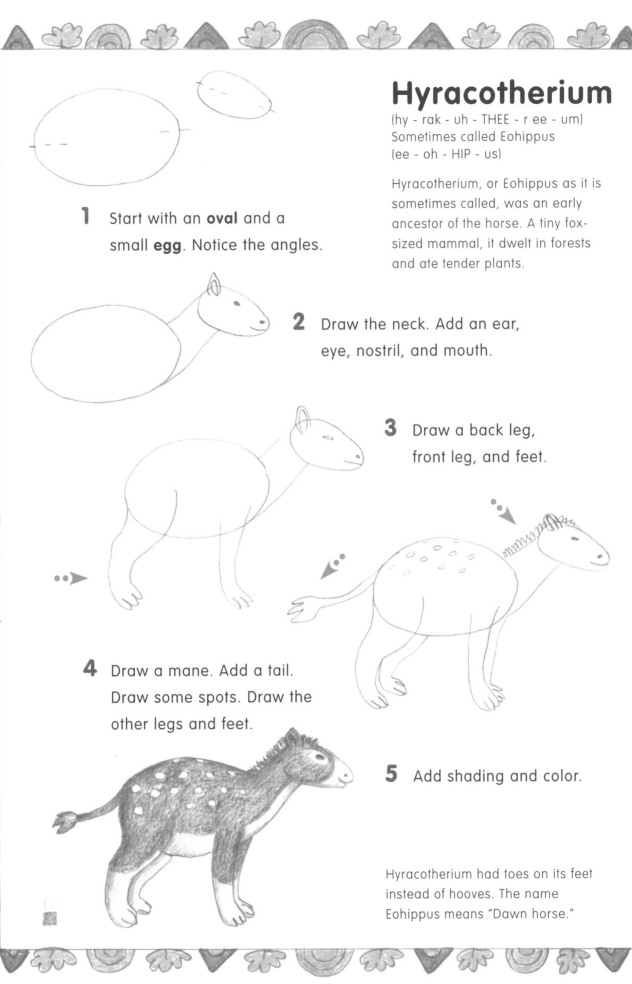

Hyracotherium

(hy - rak - uh - THEE - r ee - um)
Sometimes called Eohippus
(ee - oh - HIP - us)

Hyracotherium, or Eohippus as it is sometimes called, was an early ancestor of the horse. A tiny fox-sized mammal, it dwelt in forests and ate tender plants.

1 Start with an **oval** and a small **egg**. Notice the angles.

2 Draw the neck. Add an ear, eye, nostril, and mouth.

3 Draw a back leg, front leg, and feet.

4 Draw a mane. Add a tail. Draw some spots. Draw the other legs and feet.

5 Add shading and color.

Hyracotherium had toes on its feet instead of hooves. The name Eohippus means "Dawn horse."

Diatryma
(die - ah - TRY - ma)

Diatryma was a flightless bird, a 7-foot meat-eating terror. It was a forest dweller and probably nested on the ground.

1 Start with a big **circle** and a small **circle**.

2 Draw the neck. Add an eye. Draw tail feathers.

3 Draw an upper beak and lower beak. Begin two legs.

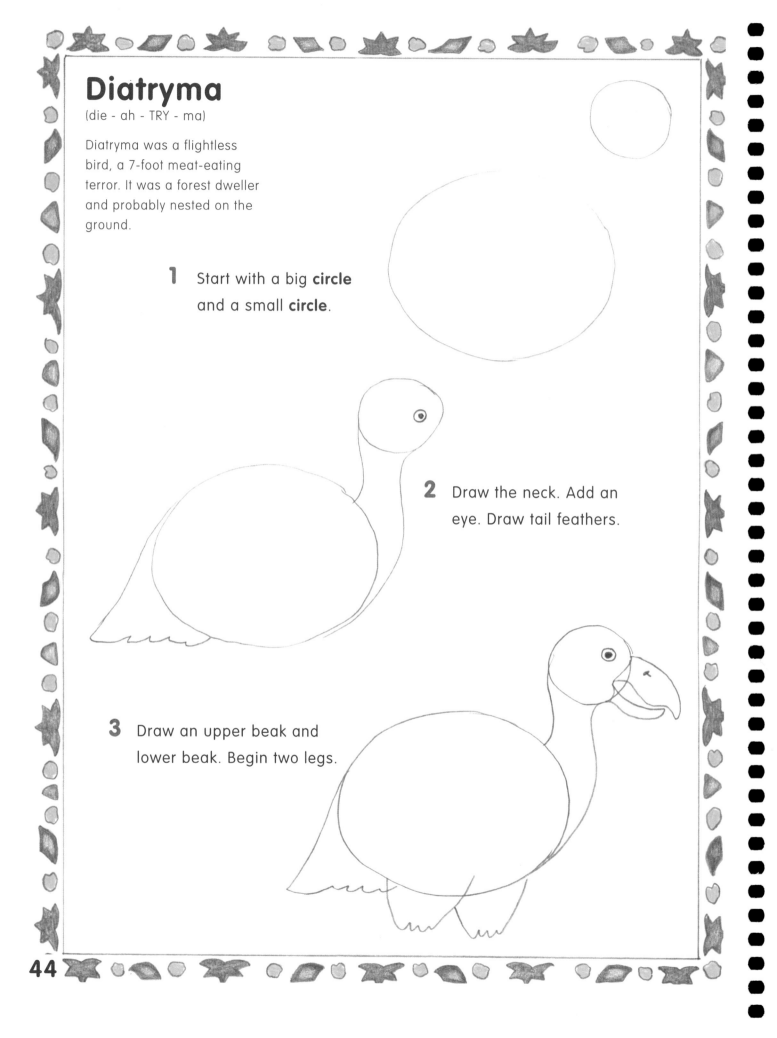

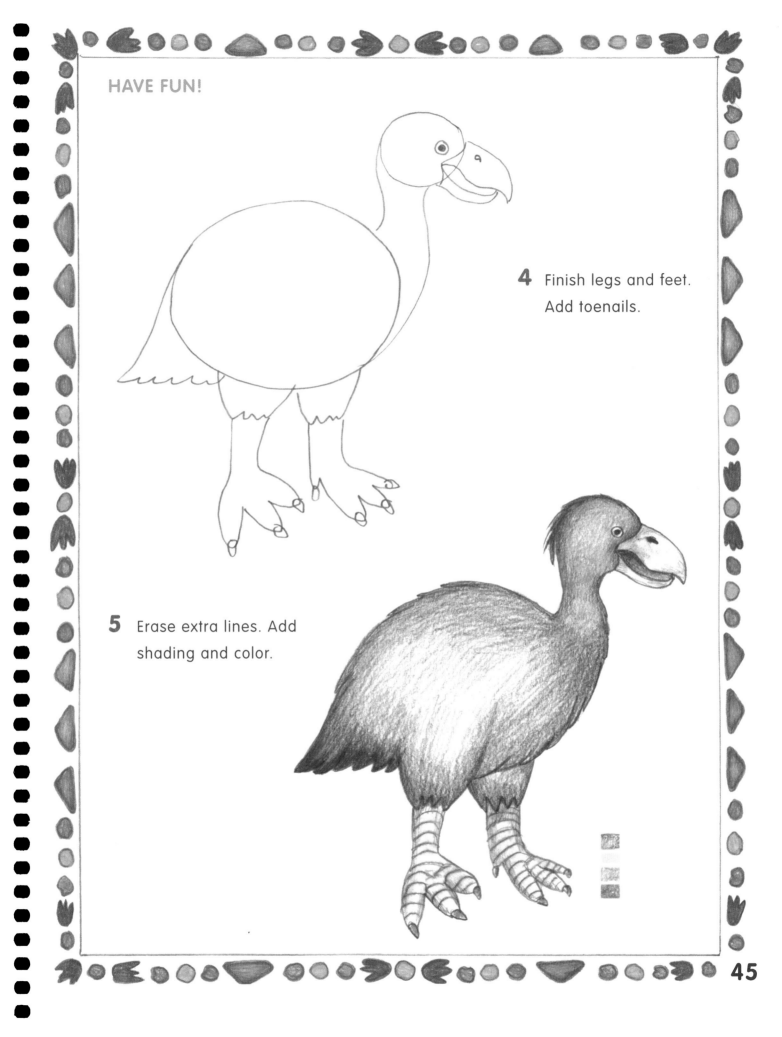

HAVE FUN!

4 Finish legs and feet. Add toenails.

5 Erase extra lines. Add shading and color.

45

Glyptodon

(GLIP - toe - don)

Glyptodon was a car-sized cousin of the modern armadillo. It was 14 feet long and 5 feet high. It had bony armor on its back and a bony helmet on its head.

1 Draw a large **oval**. Draw a small **egg** and overlap the **oval**.

2 Add an **oval** on top of head. Make an eye and nose. Draw two legs.

3 Add ears. Draw lines for armor on the head and body. Add a tail with spikes on the end. Draw toenails.

4 Erase extra lines. Add shading and color.

Woolly Mammoth

(MAM - uth)

The Woolly Mammoth was an Ice-Age mammal (see chart on page 62) that was related to the modern elephant. It lived on the edge of glaciers. Its tusks were up to 16 feet long. Whole mammoths have been found preserved in ice in Alaska and Siberia. From this, we know they had shaggy reddish-brown fur.

1 Draw three **eggs**. The big one is in the middle. Notice the angle of all the **eggs**.

2 Draw a line for the head, neck and back. Add an eye. Draw the trunk and mouth.

3 Draw a long curved tusk.
Draw two legs.

4 Draw a second curving
tusk behind the first.
Add toenails.

5 Draw the tail. Add another front and back leg. Draw zigzag lines on the belly for hair.

6 Erase extra lines. Shade and color your Woolly Mammoth. Make it shaggy!

49

Brontotherium

(BRON - toe - THEE - ree - um)

Brontotherium means "thunder beast." It weighed 5 tons and was 8 feet high. The two horns on its nose may have been used for fighting rivals during mating season.

1 Draw three **eggs**— a medium, a large, and a small one. Notice the angles.

2 Draw a curved line to connect the ovals on top and bottom. Draw an eye and a nostril.

3 Draw two horns. Draw a front leg. Draw a back leg.

PRACTICE MAKES BETTER!

4 Draw an ear. Shape the mouth. Draw a tail. Add two more legs. Draw toenails.

5 Erase extra lines. Add shading and color.

51

Megatherium

(meg - ah - THEE - ree - um)

Megatherium was a giant ground sloth. It was a slow-moving relative of today's tree sloth. About the size of an elephant, Megatherium had bony protective plates under its fur. It died out about 10,000 years ago.

1 Start with a big **egg** and a small **egg**.

2 Draw the neck. Add the tail.

3 Draw an ear. Add an eye. Shape the face.

4 Draw two front legs with big curving claws. Draw two back legs with claws.

5 Erase extra lines. Add shading and color.

53

Smilodon

(SMY - lo - don)

Smilodon is also known as a "saber toothed tiger." Its fangs were razor sharp and 6 inches long. Smilodon died out about 10,000 years ago. We don't know if it had stripes or spots. So why not make some of both?

1 Draw three **eggs**. The first one is the smallest. Notice the angles.

2 Draw curved lines on the top and bottom to connect the ovals. Shape face and jaw.

3 Add the eye and nose. Draw BIG fangs. Draw a front and back leg. Add the tail.

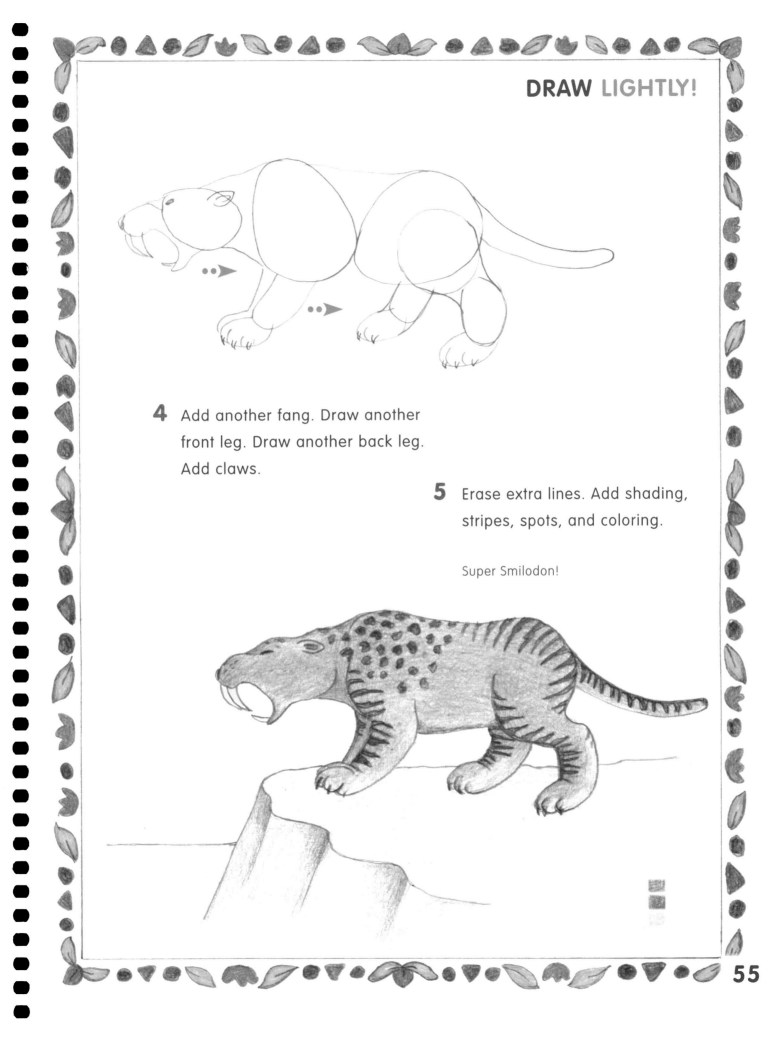

4 Add another fang. Draw another front leg. Draw another back leg. Add claws.

5 Erase extra lines. Add shading, stripes, spots, and coloring.

Super Smilodon!

Megaceros

(mee - GAS - er - us)

Megaceros was also called "Irish Elk."
Many well-preserved specimens were
found in peat bogs in Ireland.
Megaceros died out a few thousand
years ago. It had a 12-foot antler span.

1 Start with a small **egg** and a big **egg**.

2 Draw a curved neck. Draw a straight front leg, and a back leg in two sections.

6

3 Draw an eye. Add an ear. Draw another front and back leg.

4 Draw his fancy 12-foot antlers. Add hooves. Draw a tail.

5 Erase extra lines. Add shading and color.

57

Baluchitherium

(ba - LUKE - uh - thee - ree - um)

Baluchitherium was just gigantic. It was the largest land mammal that ever lived. It weighed 20 tons—equal to five elephants. It's related to the modern-day rhinoceros. It ate leaves and twigs—a lot of them!

The name Baluchitherium comes from the old name of the country Pakistan. It was called Baluchistan and that was where this fossil was found in 1911.

1 Draw a VERY big **circle** and a small **oval**.

2 Draw the neck. Add two ears. Shape the face. Draw an eye. Draw a back and front leg.

3 Add a nose and mouth.
Draw another front leg.
Draw another back leg.
Add toenails. Draw the tail.

This diagram shows how big
Baluchitherium was compared
with a modern-day elephant.

4 Erase extra lines. Add
shading and color.

Create Your Own Dinosaurs

These creatures are so fantastic and strange. It would be fun to make up your own dinosaurs and give them a crazy name.

Here are some ideas. What do you think they ate? Where did they live?

shortodon

bizarrosaurus

Drawings on these pages by Daniel Levin.

Draw an environment for your dinosaur!

Polkasaurus?

61

Time Line
When did they live?

Mezosoic Era:

Triassic period:
Morganucodon

Jurassic period:
Stegosaurus
Diplodocus
Kentrosaurus
Archaeopteryx
Compsognathus
Ichthyosaurus

Cretaceous:
Deinonychus
Triceratops
Tyrannosaurus
Maiasaurus
Iguanodon
Pachycephalosaurus
Spinosaurus
Lambeosaurus
Psittacosaurus
Velociraptor
Ankylosaurus
Pteranodon
Gallimimus
Elasmosaurus
Parasaurolophus

Cenozoic Era:

Ecocene:
Hyracotherium (Eohippus)
Diatryma

Oligocene:
Baluchitherium
Brontotherium

Pleistocene:
Megatherium
Smilodon
Megaceros
Glyptodon
Woolly Mammoth

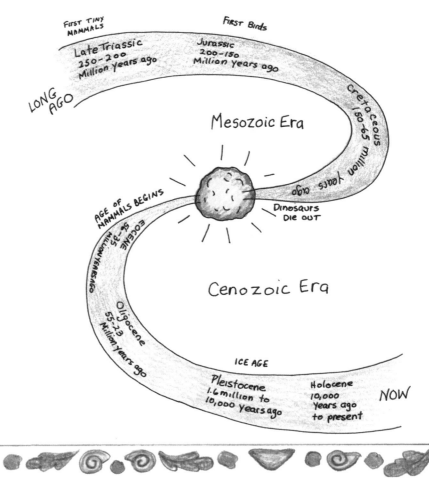

62

Good Bye Dinosaurs, Hello Mammals

Dinosaurs ruled the Earth for 160 million years. They died out on every continent around 60 million years ago. Scientists believe that a giant meteor crashed into the area that is now Central America. The dust and debris from this event clouded the sun and caused climate changes. The dinosaurs could not adapt to the changes and in a fairly short amount of time, they all disappeared.

Mammals were not affected the same way. The first mammals appeared during the late Triassic period. They were little shrew-like creatures. They were active at night and ate leaves and insects. When the dinosaurs were gone, they emerged from hiding. Soon, they took over in the lands that the dinosaurs had left empty.

Birds first appeared on Earth during the Jurassic period. Archaeopteryx had feathers and wings like a bird, but teeth and claws like meat-eating dinosaurs. Scientists believe that some of the genetic material of the dinosaurs lives on in modern-day birds, their only known surviving relative.

Scientists are learning new things about dinosaurs every day, and so can you!

Index

Learn about other
drawing books online at
1-2-3-draw.com!

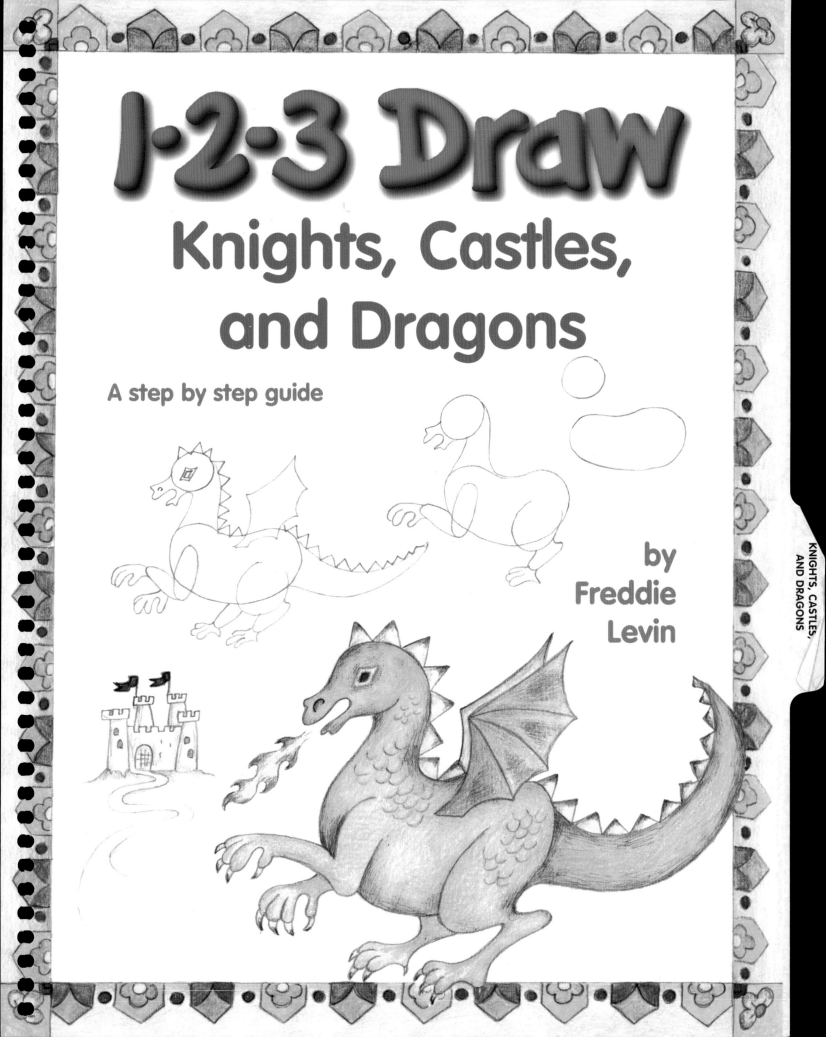

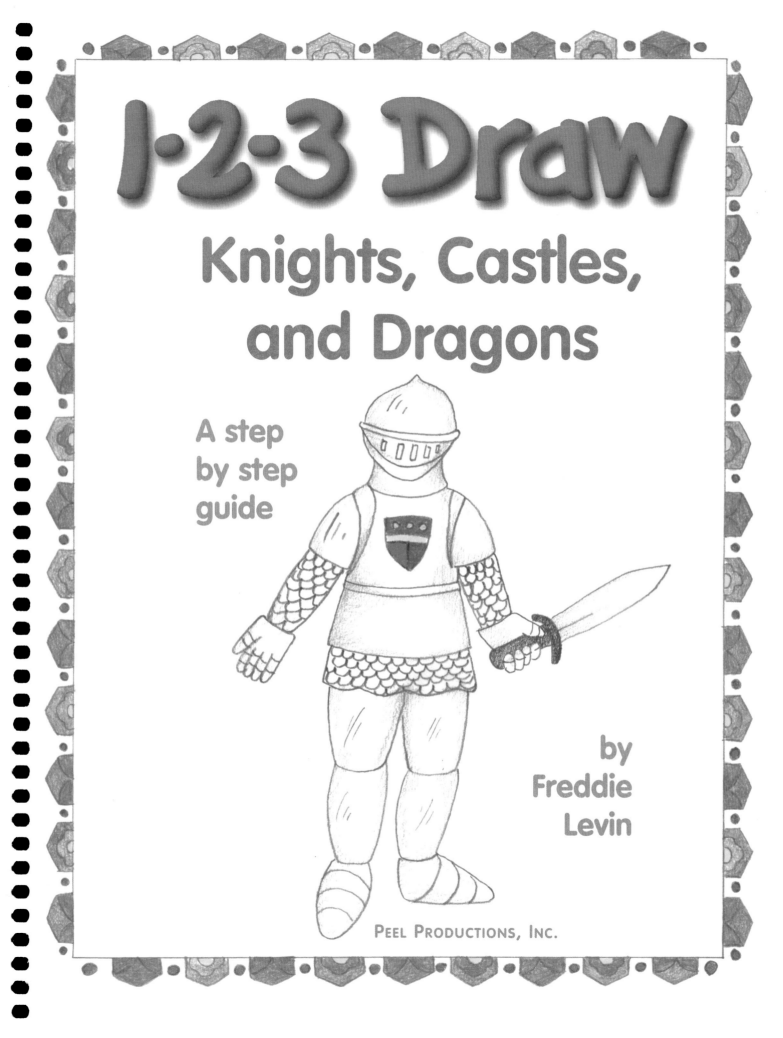

1·2·3 Draw

Knights, Castles, and Dragons

A step
by step
guide

by
Freddie
Levin

Peel Productions, Inc.

Before you begin...

You will need:

- a pencil
- an eraser
- a pencil sharpener
- a ruler for drawing straight edges
- lots of paper (recycle and re-use)
- colored pencils for finished drawings
- a folder for saving work
- a comfortable place to draw
- good light

Now let's begin...!

Published by Peel Productions, Inc.
Printed in China

Library of Congress Cataloging-in-Publication Data

Levin, Freddie.

1-2-3 draw knights, castles, and dragons: a step by step guide / by Freddie Levin. p. cm.
Includes index.
Summary: Simple instructions for drawing dragons, knights and their weapons, and castles and the people who lived in them.
ISBN 0-939217-43-0
1. Knights and knighthood in art--Juvenile literature. 2. Dragons in art--Juvenile literature. 3. Castles in art--Juvenile literature. 4. Drawing--Technique--Juvenile literature. [1. Knights and knighthood in art. 2. Dragons in art. 3. Castles in art. 4. Drawing--Technique.] I. Title: Knights, castles, and dragons. II. Title: One-two-three draw knights, castles, and dragons. III. Title.

NC825.K54 L49 2001
743'.8--dc21   2001036642Ò

Distributed to the trade and art markets in North America by

NORTH LIGHT BOOKS,
an imprint of F&W Publications, Inc.
4700 East Galbraith Road
Cincinnati, OH 45236

(800) 289-0963

Contents

Important Drawing Tips:

1 Draw lightly (SKETCH!) at first, so you can erase extra lines.

2 Practice, practice, practice.

3 Have fun drawing knights, castles

and dragons!

Basic Shapes

The drawings in this book start with three basic shapes. Learn these shapes and practice drawing them.

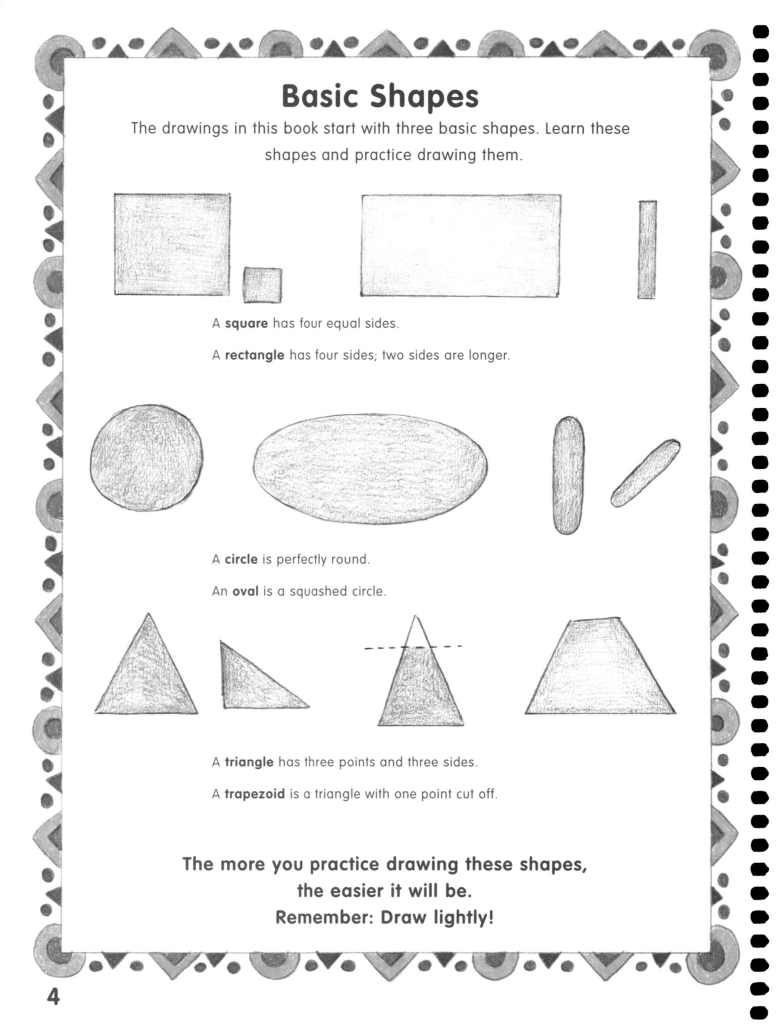

A **square** has four equal sides.

A **rectangle** has four sides; two sides are longer.

A **circle** is perfectly round.

An **oval** is a squashed circle.

A **triangle** has three points and three sides.

A **trapezoid** is a triangle with one point cut off.

**The more you practice drawing these shapes,
the easier it will be.
Remember: Draw lightly!**

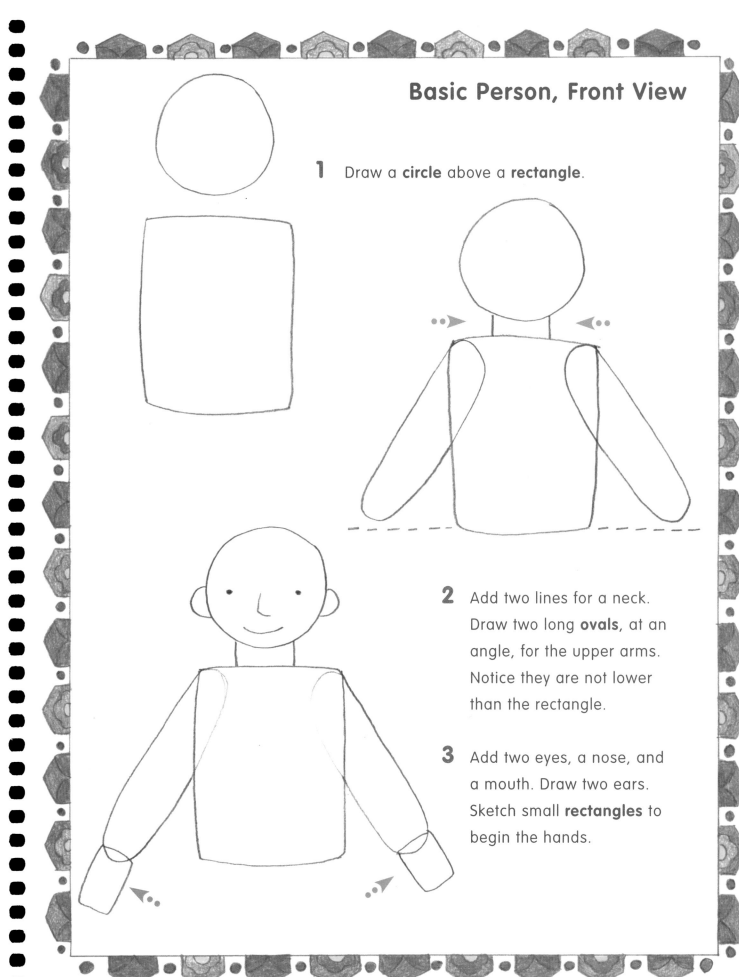

Basic Person, Front View

1 Draw a **circle** above a **rectangle**.

2 Add two lines for a neck. Draw two long **ovals**, at an angle, for the upper arms. Notice they are not lower than the rectangle.

3 Add two eyes, a nose, and a mouth. Draw two ears. Sketch small **rectangles** to begin the hands.

5

4 Draw thumbs on the hands and add lines for fingers. Sketch two long **ovals** for the legs. (The small **circles** on the arms and legs show the elbows and knees. This is good to know when you want the arms and legs to bend.)

5 Sketch **triangle** feet.

6 To finish your person, erase extra lines. The next few pages will show you how to turn the basic person into different people.

Facial Expressions:
LOOK at these different expressions! Practice drawing them.

1 sad or worried

2 angry

3 surprised

The King

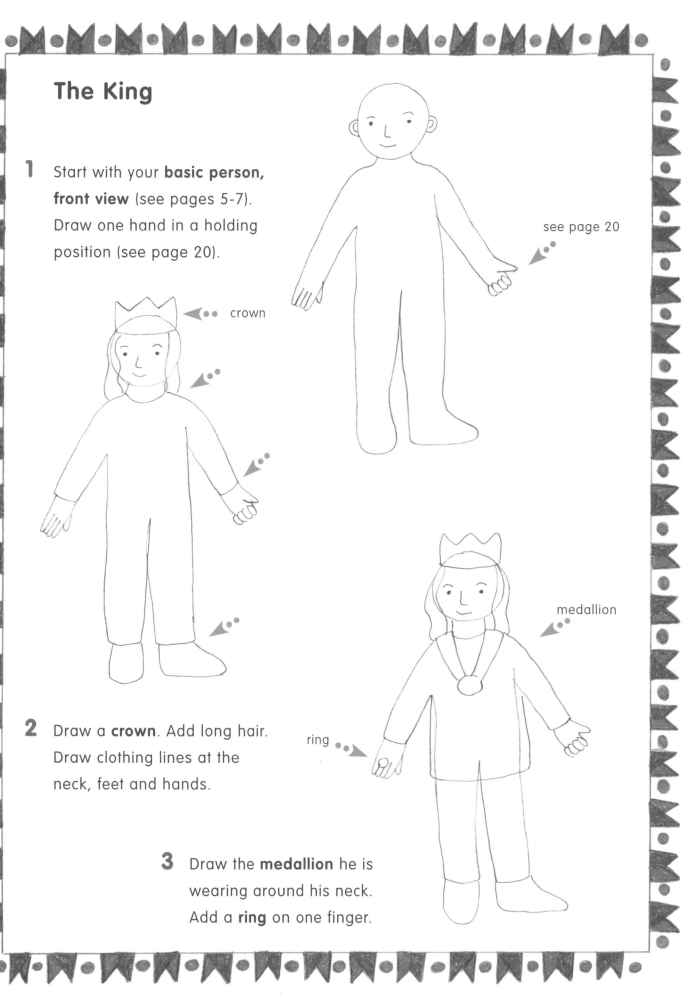

1 Start with your **basic person, front view** (see pages 5-7). Draw one hand in a holding position (see page 20).

see page 20

crown

2 Draw a **crown**. Add long hair. Draw clothing lines at the neck, feet and hands.

medallion

ring

3 Draw the **medallion** he is wearing around his neck. Add a **ring** on one finger.

4 Add jewels to the crown. Draw bushy eyebrows and a beard. Add a royal robe.

5 LOOK at the final drawing! Erase extra lines. Give him a **scepter** to hold. (The crown, the scepter, the ring, and the medallions were some of the symbols of his kingdom). Shade and color. (Purple, blue and red dyes were expensive and so were often used for royal clothing.)

scepter

During the Middle Ages (500 A.D to 1500 A.D.), Europe was divided into many small nations constantly at war. A king owned all the land in his kingdom. He gave some of his land to barons who then swore loyalty to the king. The barons helped the king fight the kings of other nations. Sometimes the king had to keep his own barons from fighting with each other. It was not easy to be a king during the Middle Ages.

Basic Person, Side View

1 Draw a **circle** above a **rectangle**.

2 Add two lines for the neck. Draw two long, thin **ovals** for the arms. Notice the angle.

3 Draw a **triangle** for the nose. Add an eye, a mouth, and an ear. Draw two **rectangles** to begin the hands.

4 Draw **triangles** for thumbs and add lines for fingers. Draw two long thin **ovals** for legs (**circles** show where elbows and knees would be).

5 Draw lines to round off the shoulders. Sketch **triangles** for feet.

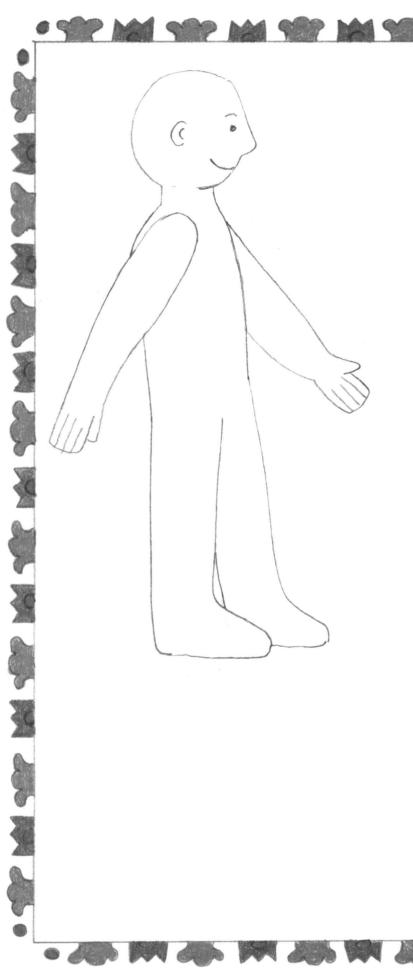

6 LOOK at the final drawing! Erase extra lines. You are now ready to turn the basic person into different people.

Facial Expressions: LOOK at these different expressions! Practice drawing them.

1 angry

2 sad

3 surprised

A Princess

A princess is the daughter of a king and queen. During the Middle Ages, she was expected to learn how to manage a large household, use herbs for medicines, embroider, dance and play a musical instrument. She had to be a gracious hostess as well.

hennin

kirtle

1 Start with your **basic person, side view** (see pages 10-12).

2 Draw a **triangular** hat called a **hennin** (HEN in). Add clothing lines at the neck and wrists. Draw a long, flowing dress called a **kirtle** (KIR till).

3 Draw a flowing scarf from the tip of the hat. Draw long wavy hair. Give the princess a bead necklace.

4 LOOK at the final drawing! Erase extra lines. Shade and color. (Royalty often wore richly decorated clothing. This princess has a kirtle of embroidered stars and satin slippers.)

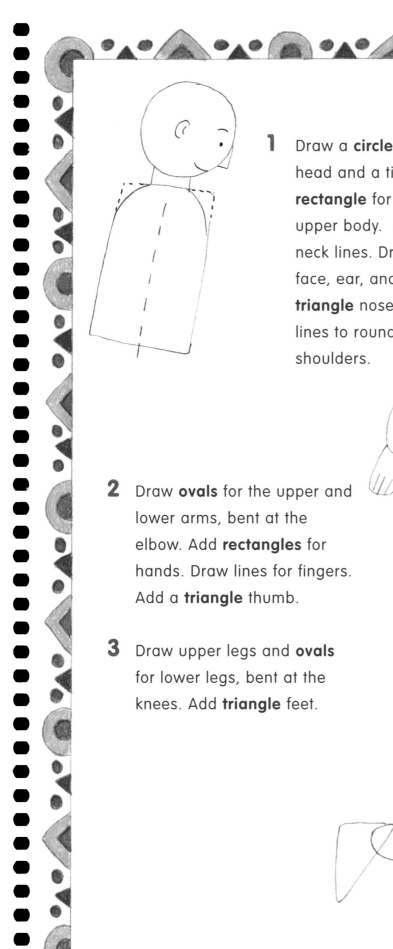

Basic Person, Running

1 Draw a **circle** for the head and a tilted **rectangle** for the upper body. Add neck lines. Draw the face, ear, and **triangle** nose. Add lines to round the shoulders.

2 Draw **ovals** for the upper and lower arms, bent at the elbow. Add **rectangles** for hands. Draw lines for fingers. Add a **triangle** thumb.

3 Draw upper legs and **ovals** for lower legs, bent at the knees. Add **triangle** feet.

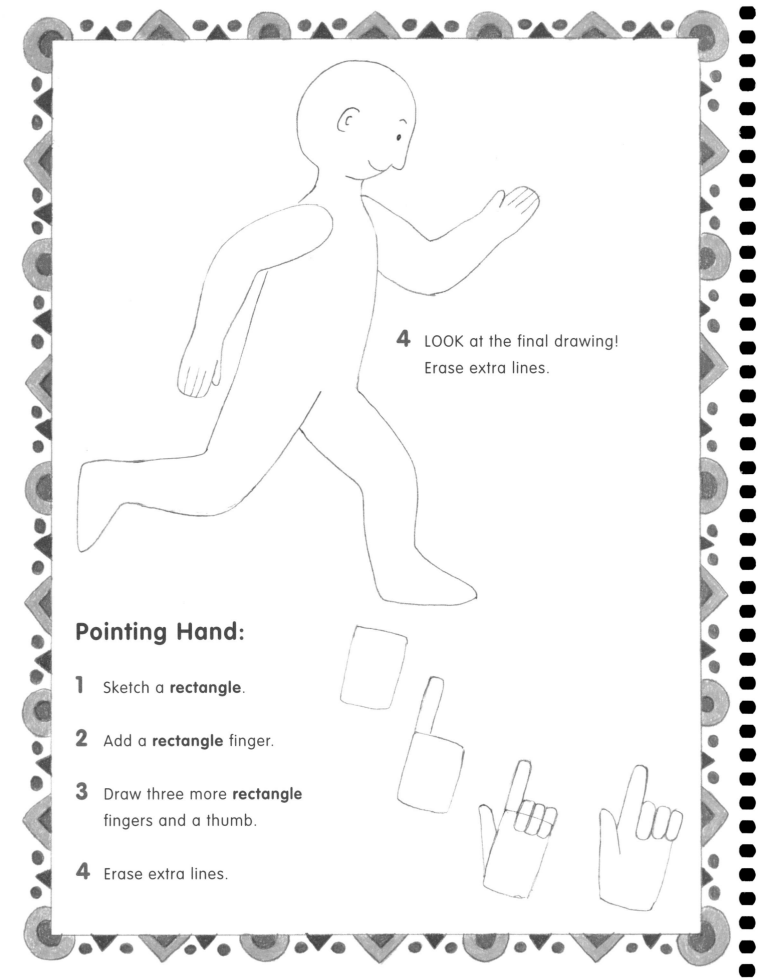

4 LOOK at the final drawing!
Erase extra lines.

Pointing Hand:

1 Sketch a **rectangle**.

2 Add a **rectangle** finger.

3 Draw three more **rectangle**
fingers and a thumb.

4 Erase extra lines.

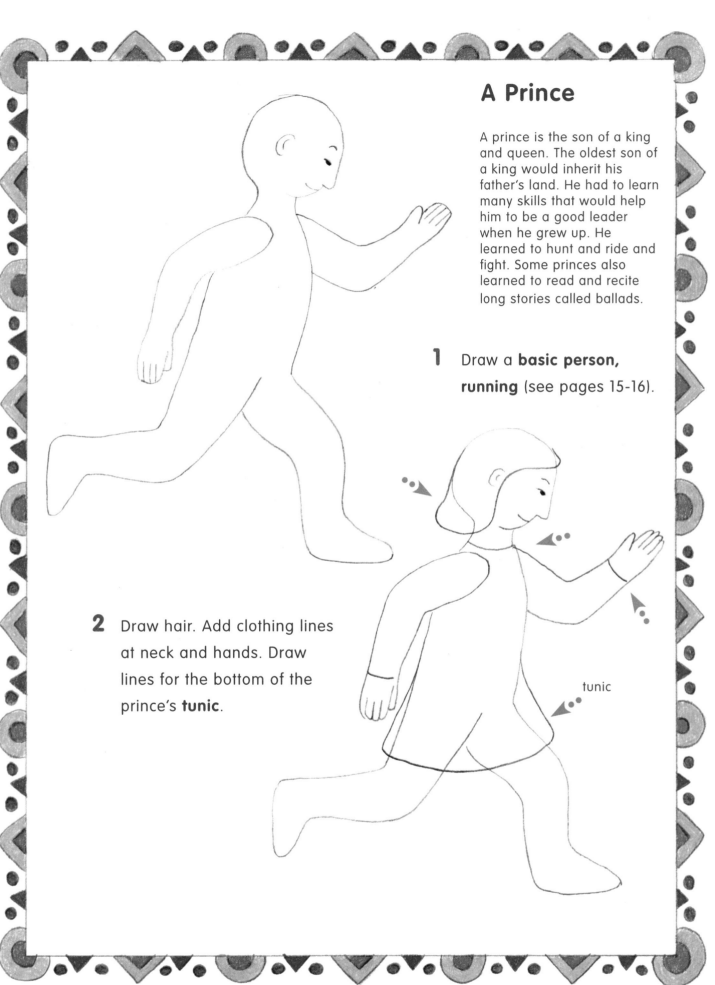

A Prince

A prince is the son of a king and queen. The oldest son of a king would inherit his father's land. He had to learn many skills that would help him to be a good leader when he grew up. He learned to hunt and ride and fight. Some princes also learned to read and recite long stories called ballads.

1 Draw a **basic person, running** (see pages 15-16).

2 Draw hair. Add clothing lines at neck and hands. Draw lines for the bottom of the prince's **tunic**.

tunic

crown

belt

3 Draw a **crown** for the prince. Add a **belt** to the tunic. Draw a clothing line near the feet.

4 LOOK at the final drawing. Erase extra lines. Add some jewels to his crown. Draw the details you see. Shade and color.

Perfect prince!

Basic Person, Sitting

1 Draw a **circle** for the head and a **rectangle** for the upper body. Add a **triangle** nose. Draw the eye, ear, and mouth. Add two lines for the neck.

2 Draw long thin **ovals** for the upper and lower arms, bending at the elbow. Add a **rectangle** for the hand. Draw a thumb and lines for fingers.

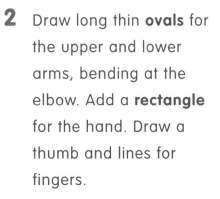

3 Draw lines to round the shoulders. Draw **ovals** for the upper and lower leg, bent at the knee. Add a **triangle** for a foot.

4 LOOK at this drawing! Erase extra lines. Draw a chair.

Hand Holding Something:

1 Start with a **rectangle**.

2 Add four small **ovals** for fingers.

3 Draw a thumb.

4 Erase extra lines. Draw a handle for the hand to hold.

The Queen

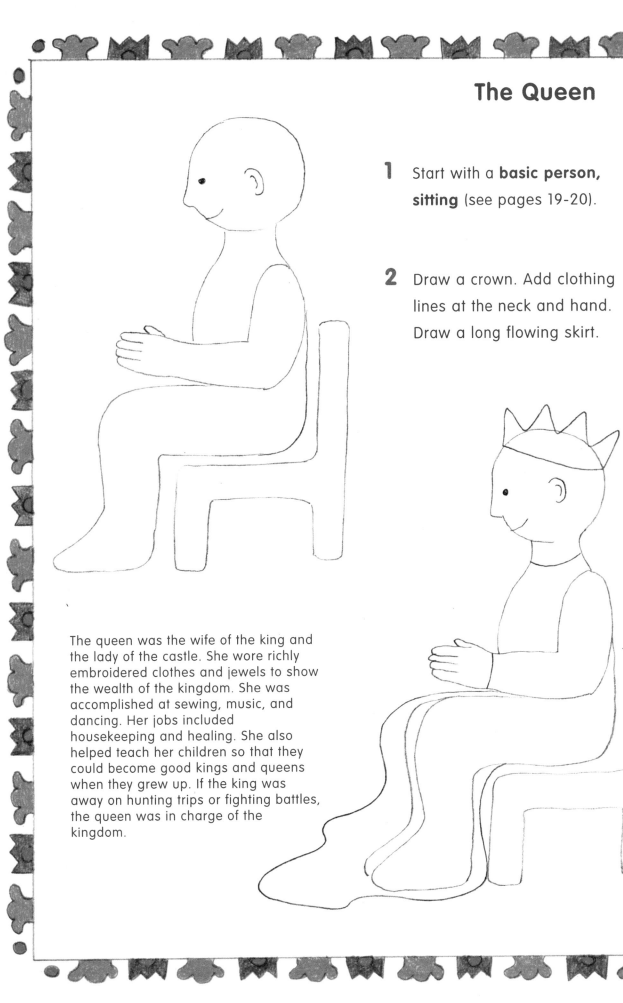

1 Start with a **basic person, sitting** (see pages 19-20).

2 Draw a crown. Add clothing lines at the neck and hand. Draw a long flowing skirt.

The queen was the wife of the king and the lady of the castle. She wore richly embroidered clothes and jewels to show the wealth of the kingdom. She was accomplished at sewing, music, and dancing. Her jobs included housekeeping and healing. She also helped teach her children so that they could become good kings and queens when they grew up. If the king was away on hunting trips or fighting battles, the queen was in charge of the kingdom.

3 Draw her curly hair. Add a ring. Add lines to change the chair into a throne by making the back taller and the feet bigger.

4 LOOK at the final drawing! Erase extra lines. Add jewels to her crown. Give her a necklace. Decorate the throne with jewels. Shade and color.

Castle One

Stone castles in Europe date from the 11th century. The name castle comes from the Latin word for fort or stronghold. Some were luxurious and fancy to show off the wealth of the king, but some were as bare and cold as a cave.

1 Draw two connecting **rectangles**. You may want to use a ruler to keep your lines straight.

2 Add two connecting **rectangles** on the left side. Notice, the lower **rectangle** is slightly wider.

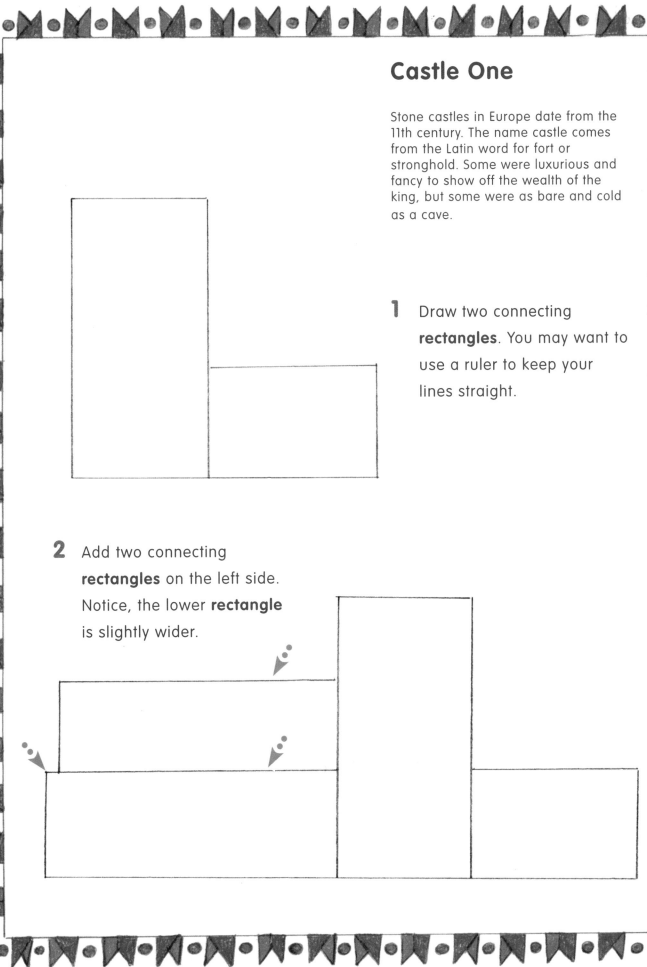

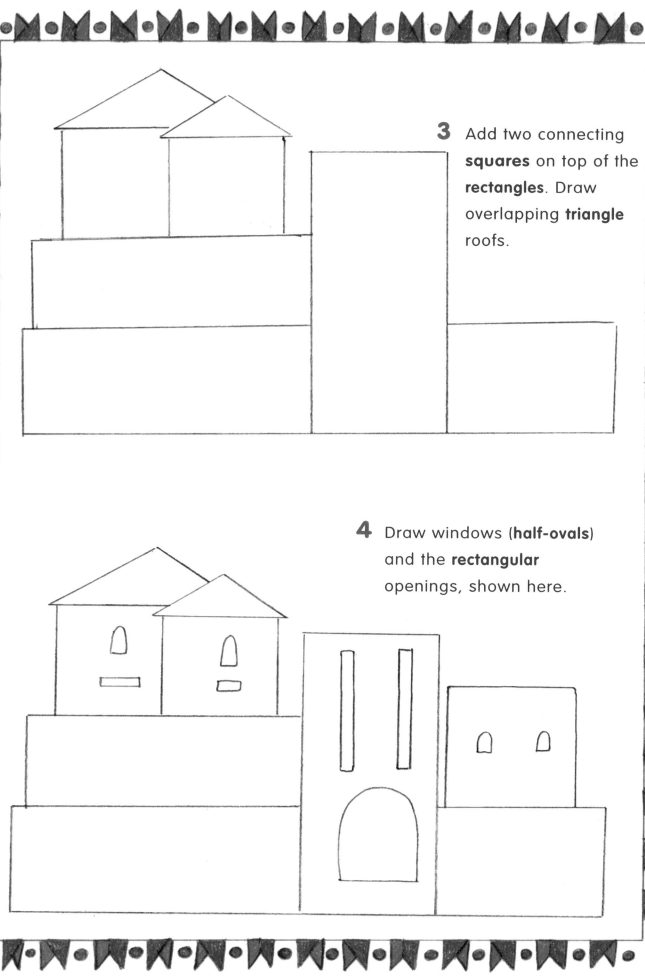

3 Add two connecting **squares** on top of the **rectangles**. Draw overlapping **triangle** roofs.

4 Draw windows (**half-ovals**) and the **rectangular** openings, shown here.

24

5 Add three more **rectangular** shapes. Draw more windows. Add iron bars (**portcullis**) to the main gate. The portcullis covers the main entrance to the castle and prevents the entrance of an enemy.

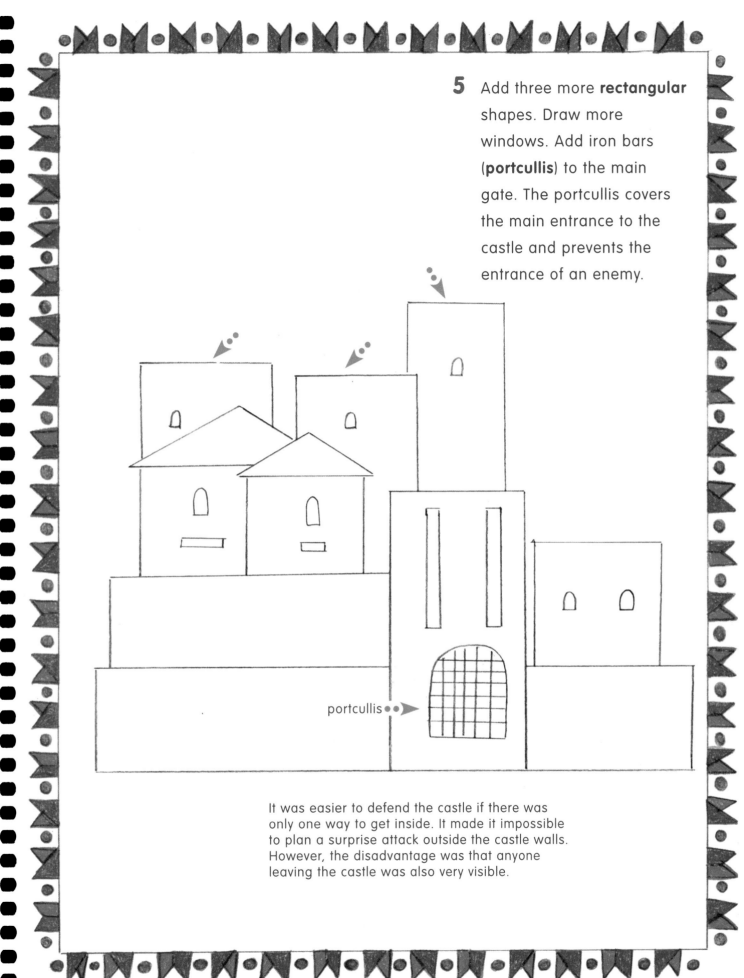

portcullis

It was easier to defend the castle if there was only one way to get inside. It made it impossible to plan a surprise attack outside the castle walls. However, the disadvantage was that anyone leaving the castle was also very visible.

6 Draw **crenelations** and **machicolations** on the castle towers. Add a road coming out of the main gate. Leave a space for the **moat**.

The forms on top of a castle tower are called **crenelations** (kren a LAY shuns). They allowed soldiers to aim down at the enemy and still have the protection of the stone walls. The overhanging openings underneath the crenelation are called **machicolations** (ma CHIK a LAY shuns) and they served the same purpose.

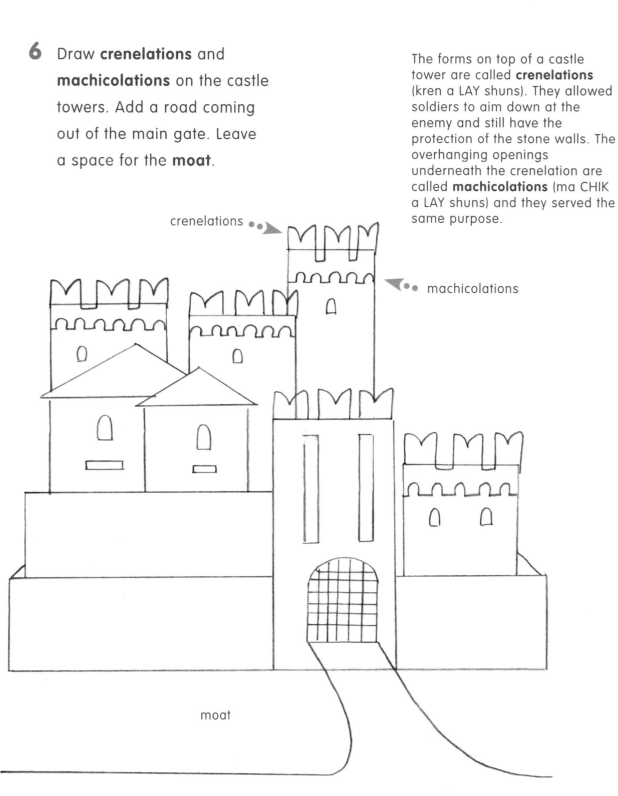

crenelations

machicolations

moat

A moat was a ditch that was dug around the castle and filled with water. The only way to get to the main gate was over a bridge. The moat kept soldiers from getting close to the castle walls.

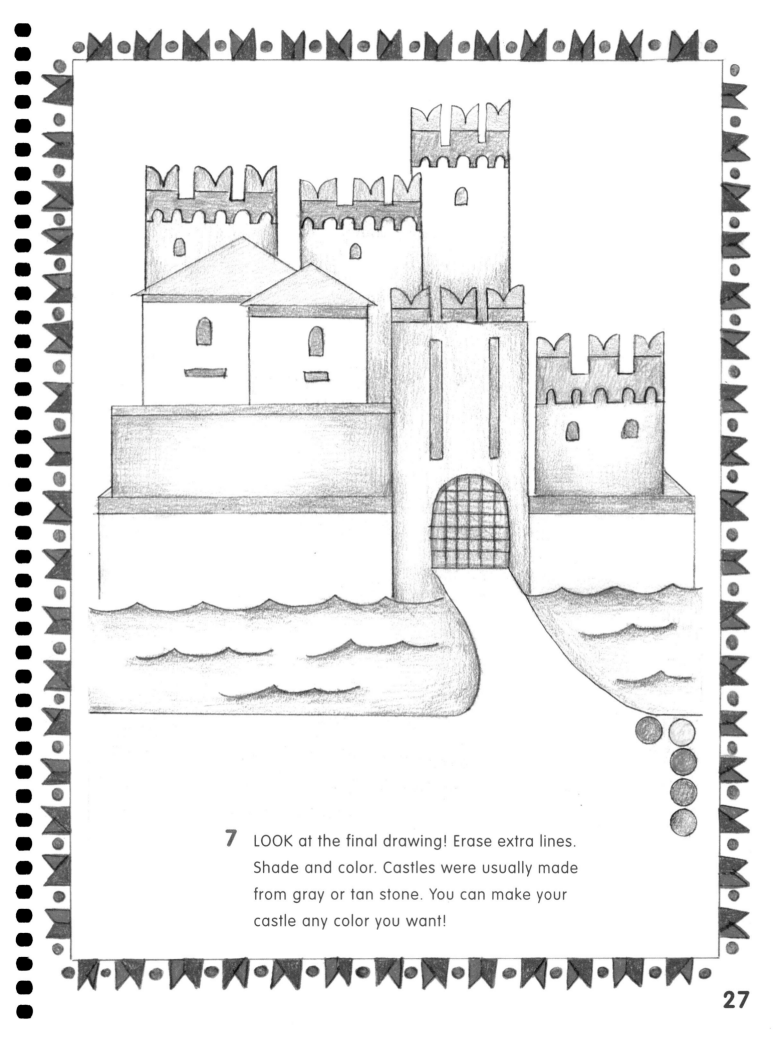

7 LOOK at the final drawing! Erase extra lines. Shade and color. Castles were usually made from gray or tan stone. You can make your castle any color you want!

Castle Two

Castles were built on foundations of natural rock. When a ditch or moat was dug, the rock was used to build the castle walls which were often eight feet thick or more. The roofs of the towers were made of sheets of lead because it was fireproof. Sometimes as many as 3,000 workers were employed to build the castle.

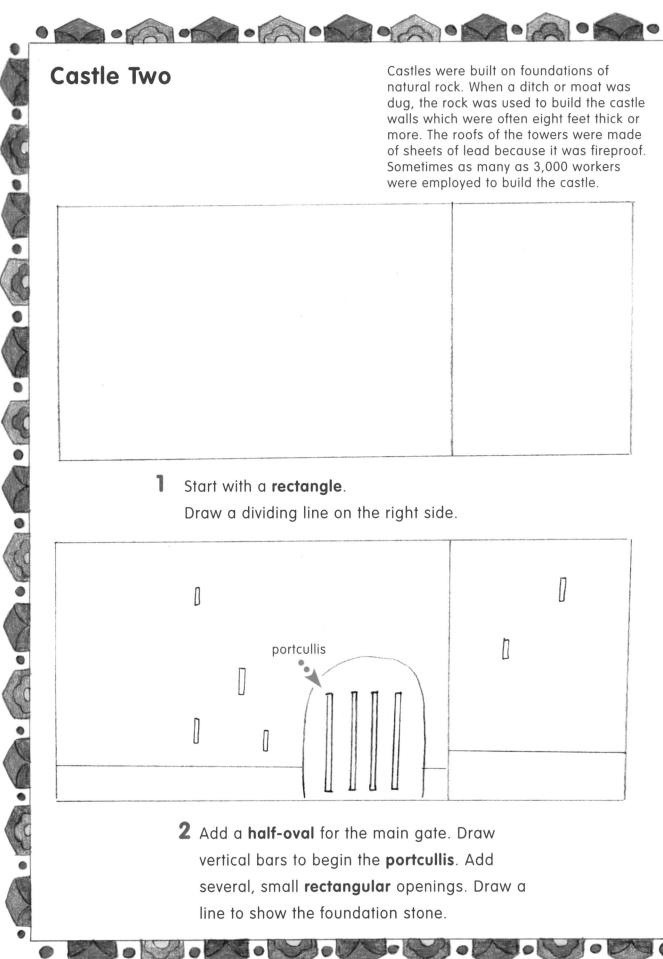

1 Start with a **rectangle**.

Draw a dividing line on the right side.

portcullis

2 Add a **half-oval** for the main gate. Draw vertical bars to begin the **portcullis**. Add several, small **rectangular** openings. Draw a line to show the foundation stone.

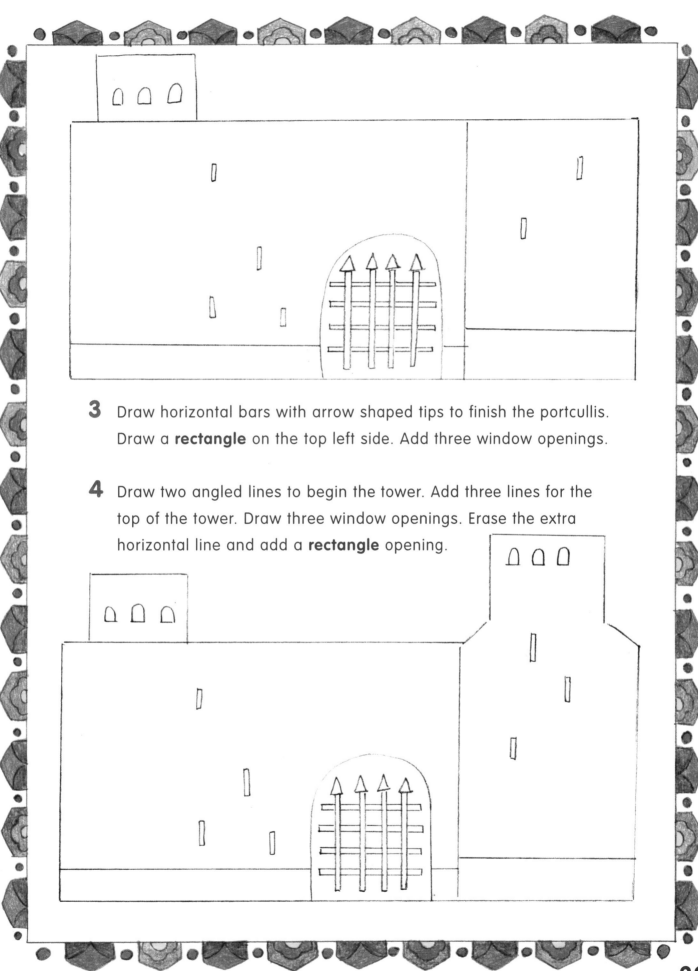

3 Draw horizontal bars with arrow shaped tips to finish the portcullis. Draw a **rectangle** on the top left side. Add three window openings.

4 Draw two angled lines to begin the tower. Add three lines for the top of the tower. Draw three window openings. Erase the extra horizontal line and add a **rectangle** opening.

5 Draw three tall **rectangles** starting on the left. Add a **triangle** roof to the one above the gate. Draw a **square** on top of the tower.

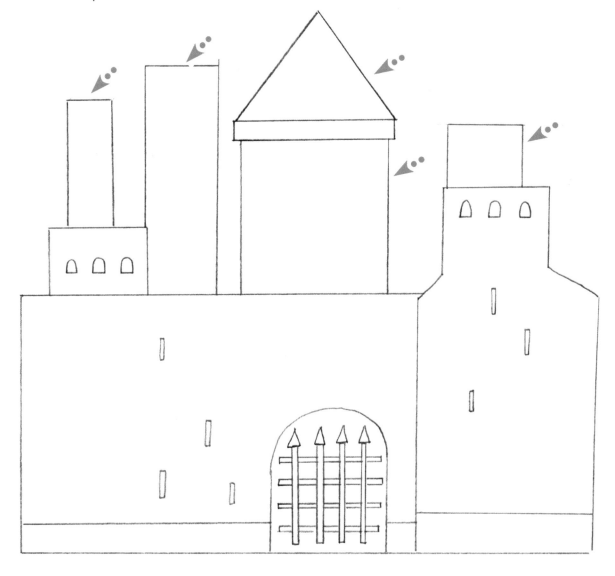

The place in the middle of the castle, where people lived, was called the "keep." It was higher than the surrounding walls. Inside, it was often decorated with richly colored weavings called 'tapestries' and beautifully carved stone.

6 Draw a **rectangular** tower behind the keep. Draw another **rectangular** tower to the right of the keep. On top of each tower, draw a **rectangle**. Add a line between the second tower and the keep. Draw all the windows and openings you see.

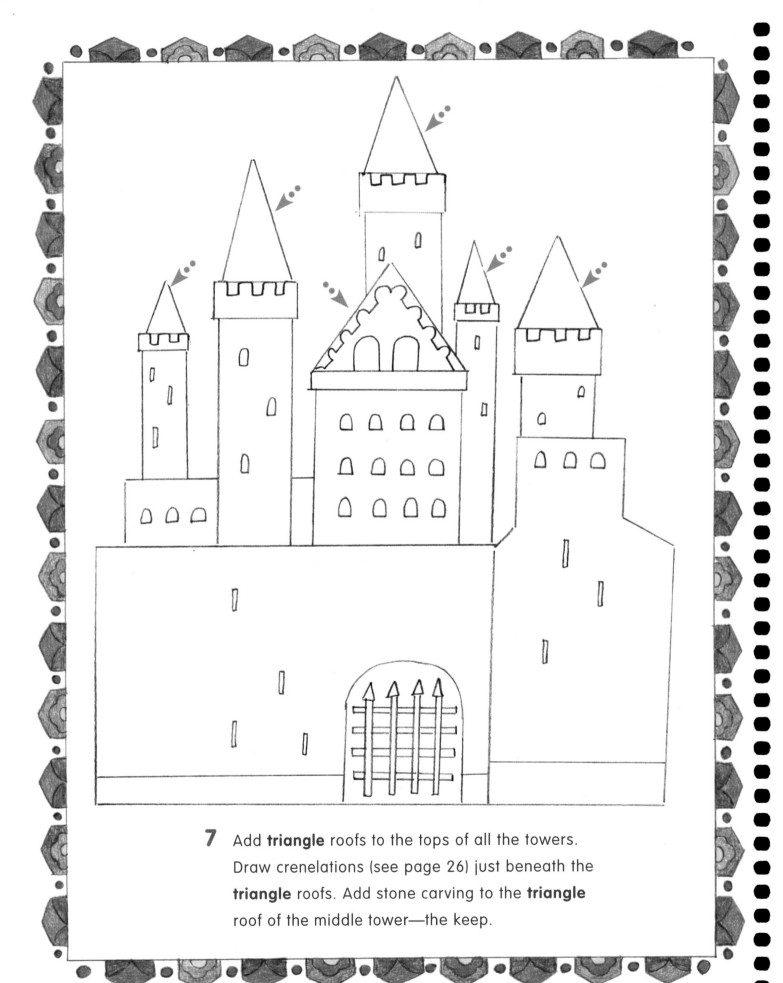

7 Add **triangle** roofs to the tops of all the towers. Draw crenelations (see page 26) just beneath the **triangle** roofs. Add stone carving to the **triangle** roof of the middle tower—the keep.

8 LOOK at the final drawing! Erase extra lines. Shade and color. Remember that even though most real castles were made of gray or tan stone, you can make your castle any color you want.

Cool castle!

Swan

Make a swan to swim in your castle moat!

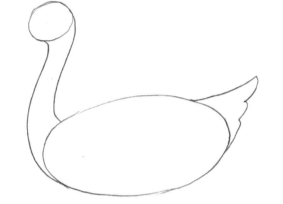

1 Sketch a **circle** for the head and an **oval** for the body.

2 Connect the **circle** and the **oval** with curving neck lines. Add tail feathers.

3 Draw an eye and a beak. Add a wing line.

4 Erase extra lines. Shade and color your swan.

Heraldry

During the Middle Ages, most people could not read. A man in a full suit of armor was not easy to identify. So each family designed a unique shield or crest. A man would wear it on the coat that covered his armor and this became his **coat of arms**. Heraldry is the study of coats of arms and family histories. These are some of the designs that were used in heraldry. Can you design one for yourself or your family?

Diagonal Stripes

Chevron Stripe

Checks

Flowers and Dots (rondels)

Chevron and Leaf

Wavy lines

Diagonal Stripe and Crowns

Dragon

A Knight

A knight was a warrior or a soldier. He rode a horse and wore metal armor. The armor was very costly and heavy and, worst of all, it was very hot. Over the years, styles of armor changed. Some knights wore combinations of chain mail (fabric made of small metal links), plated armor, and hardened leather. As time went on, less leather and chain mail were used until the whole suit was made of interconnected plates of metal. It had to be made exactly to the measurements of the man who was going to wear it.

helmet

tunic

1 Start with a drawing of a **basic person, front view** (see pages 5-7). Make his left hand in the holding position.

2 Draw the **helmet** with the visor down. Draw the **tunic**.

3 Draw shoulder plates. Add a belt around the tunic. Draw the metal plated gloves and finger joint lines. (The joints made it possible for the fingers to move.)

4 Draw chain mail on his arms and below his tunic. Draw the handle to his broad sword in his left hand. Add armor thigh covers. Draw a line at the ankle where his metal boots begin.

5 LOOK at the final drawing! Erase extra lines. Draw the coat of arms on his tunic. Add other details you see. Don't forget his broad sword and his boot plates—they made it possible for him to move his feet.

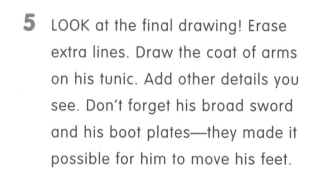

gauntlet

cuisse

hauberk

The armored gloves are called **gauntlets** (GAWNT lets).

The armored thigh coverings are called **cuisse** (KWEES).

The tunic of chain mail is called a **hauberk** (HO burk).

Horse

A knight's horse had to be big and sturdy to carry a man and all his armor into battle. Sometimes the horse also wore coat of arms and specially made armor. A well trained, valiant horse was an asset to a knight and highly valued.

1 Sketch a small **circle** for the horse's head. Sketch a big **oval** for the body.

2 Draw curved lines for the neck. Add the nose and mouth.

3 Draw two ears, an eye, and a nostril. Draw the flowing tail.

4 Draw a front and a back leg.

5 Add another front leg and another back leg. Draw a line for the hooves.

40

bridle

reins

6 Draw the **reins** and **bridle**.

7 Add a **saddle**. Erase extra lines.

saddle

You can shade and color your horse,
or wait and add a rider. (Pages 42
through 44 show you how to draw a
knight riding your horse.)

Knight on Horseback

1 To start your knight, draw a **circle** for a head. Notice how far above the horse's ears the head is. Draw a **half-oval** for the chest and a small **half-oval** for the shoulder.

2 Add two **ovals** for the upper and lower arm, bent at the elbow. Draw two **ovals** for the upper and lower leg, bent at the knee.

helmet

3 Draw a **helmet** on the knight's head.
Draw a hand holding the reins. Draw feet.

4 LOOK at the final drawing! Erase extra lines. Draw a scene. (The castle in the background is on pages 28-33.) Shade and color.

44

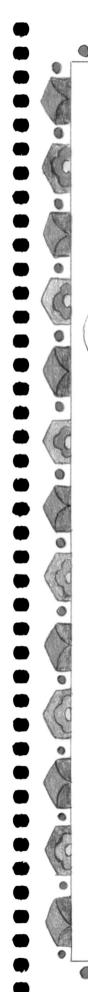

Standing Dragon

1 Sketch a small **circle** for the dragon's head. Sketch a large **oval** for its body.

2 Add curving neck lines. Draw a nose and mouth.

3 Draw spiky scales down his neck. Draw a diamond shaped eye. Add a nostril.

The people of the Middle Ages believed many things that we do not. They believed that the Earth was flat and that the sun revolved around the Earth. They believed in the existence of the huge, fire-breathing reptiles called dragons. Many stories were told of brave knights who battled dragons to save villages, castles, or princesses.

4 Draw a front leg. Draw a back leg. Add a curving tail.

5 Draw a front foot. Draw a back foot. Add spiky scales to the long tail.

6 Draw a wing. Draw another front foot. Draw another back leg and foot.

7 Draw another wing. Add lines to the first wing. Draw claws on all four feet.

8 Draw fire coming out of his mouth. Add lines on his neck, belly and tail. Draw lots of scales on your dragon.

9 LOOK at the final drawing! Erase extra lines. Shade and color your dragon.

Dragons are imaginary and can be any color you want them to be!

Dynamite dragon!

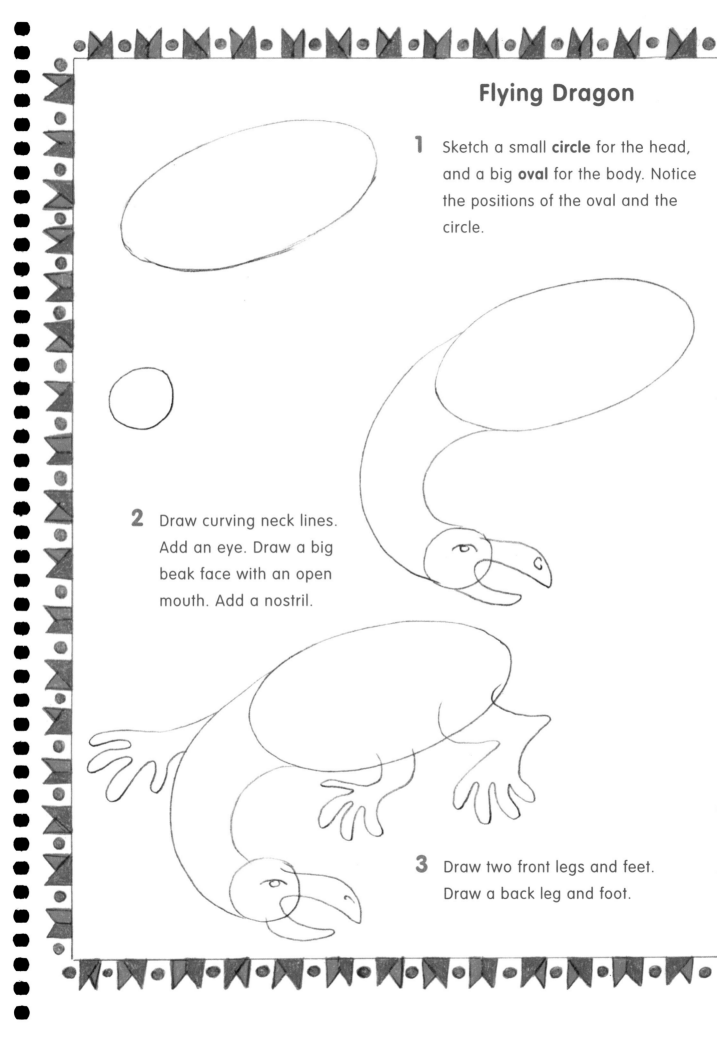

Flying Dragon

1 Sketch a small **circle** for the head, and a big **oval** for the body. Notice the positions of the oval and the circle.

2 Draw curving neck lines. Add an eye. Draw a big beak face with an open mouth. Add a nostril.

3 Draw two front legs and feet. Draw a back leg and foot.

4 Draw two wings on its back. Add a barbed tail. Draw claws on all the feet. Put horns on the dragon's head.

5 Add rib lines to the wings. Draw spiky scales down the neck and tail. Make fire coming out of the dragon's mouth!

6 LOOK at the final drawing! Erase extra lines. Add details. Shade and color your dragon. Make a background scene with a knight battling the dragon!

Weapons

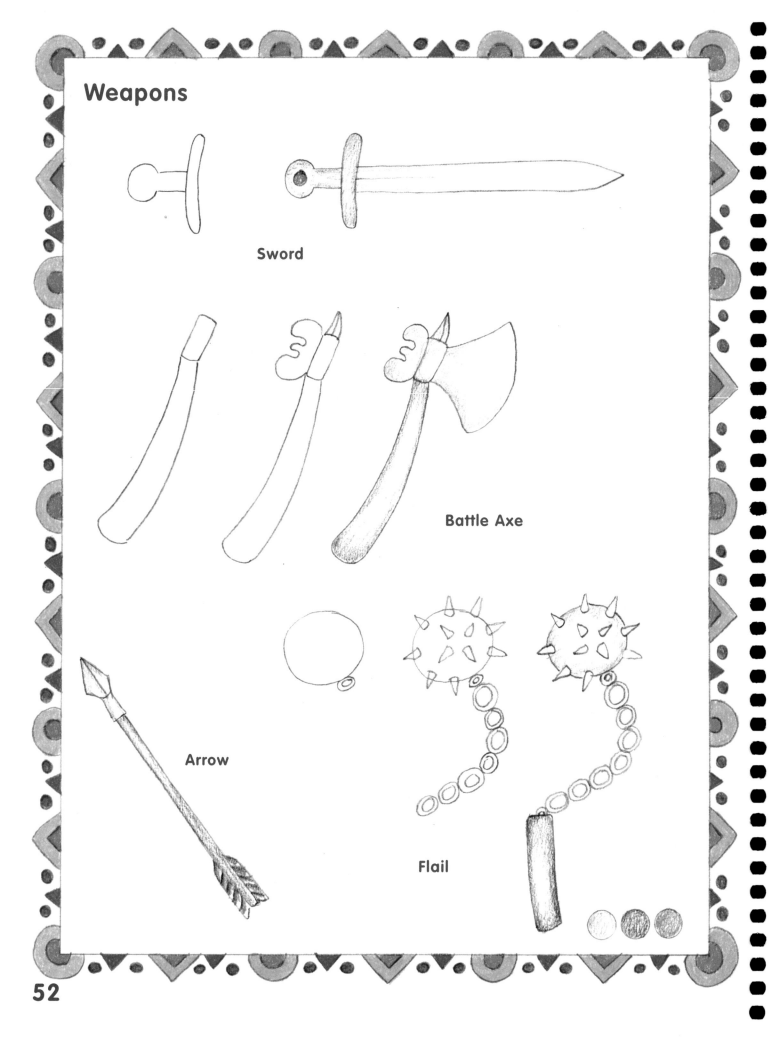

Sword

Battle Axe

Arrow

Flail

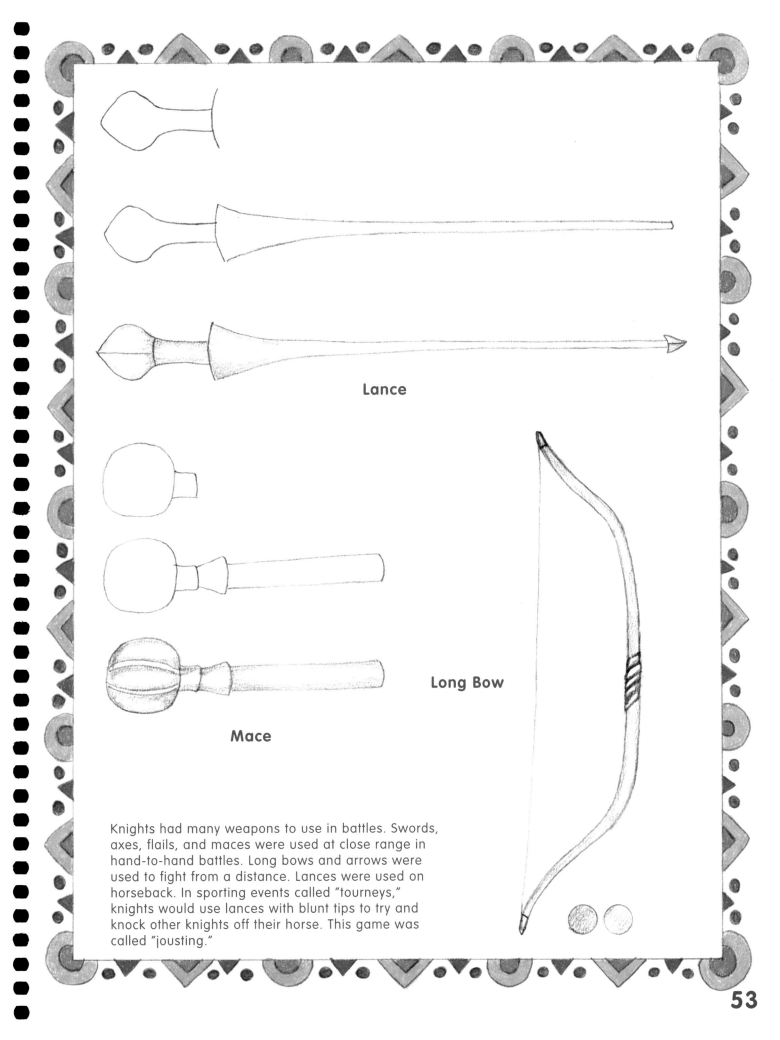

Lance

Long Bow

Mace

Knights had many weapons to use in battles. Swords, axes, flails, and maces were used at close range in hand-to-hand battles. Long bows and arrows were used to fight from a distance. Lances were used on horseback. In sporting events called "tourneys," knights would use lances with blunt tips to try and knock other knights off their horse. This game was called "jousting."

Falconry

1 Sketch a **circle** and an **oval**. Add an eye.

2 Draw a beak and two folded wings.

3 Add feet and a branch.

4 LOOK at the final drawing! Draw a hood over the hawk's head. Add markings to the wings. Add claws to the feet. Erase extra lines. Shade and color.

A falconer was an expert in training birds to hunt. Falcons, hawks, and other birds of prey were specially trained. The hood on the bird's head was part of the training—it kept the bird calm. Ladies and knights would keep their favorite hawk or falcon with them and let the birds sit on the backs of their chairs during dinner.

A Page

At the age of seven, a knight's son was sent away to another castle to begin his training for knighthood. He was called a "page" and he had many duties. At mealtime, he carved meats and served the lords and ladies of the castles. He had to learn manners and how to behave respectfully. He practiced fighting skills with wooden swords. He mastered riding horses and shooting bows and arrows.

1 Start with a **basic person running** (see pages 15-16).

2 Draw a hat and hair. Add clothing lines at the neck and hands. Draw his **tunic** with short sleeves.

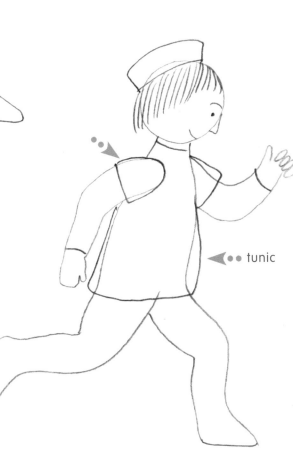

tunic

belt

3 Draw a **belt** on his tunic.
Draw a bow and arrow in
his hands. Draw lines and
laces at the top of his
shoes.

4 LOOK at the final drawing!
Erase extra lines.
Add details. Shade and
color.

A Squire

When a page turned fourteen, he became a squire. He was the personal servant of a knight and traveled with him. He had many duties including cleaning and caring for the knight's armor. He had to learn to wear heavy armor and he had training in fighting skills. When he was eighteen years old, he could become a knight in a ceremony called "dubbing."

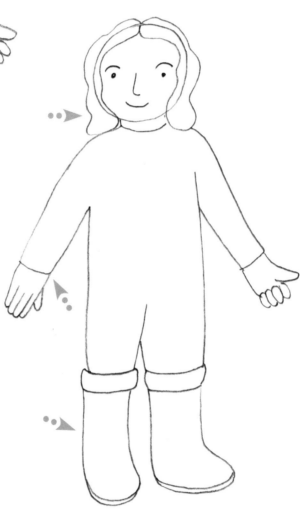

1 Start with a **basic person, front view** (see pages 5-7).

2 Draw hair lines. Add clothing lines at the neck and wrists. Draw the squire's big boots.

tunic

3 Draw his **tunic**. Add a **belt**.

4 LOOK at the final drawing. Erase extra lines. Give him a sword and shield. Add details. Don't forget his coat of arms. Shade and color.

A Minstrel

A minstrel was a traveling musician. He told stories and sang songs called ballads. Since most people in the Middle Ages could not read, this was a way they could hear stories and poems. Minstrels played many instruments including lutes, pipes, drums, and harps.

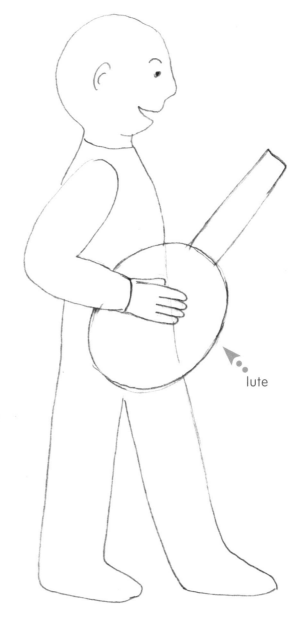

lute

1 Start with a **basic person, side view** (see pages 10-12).

2 Draw an **oval** and a **rectangle** to begin the minstrel's **lute**.

3 Draw a small **circle** inside the **oval** of the lute. Draw the tip of the neck. Add four small round pegs.

4 LOOK at the final drawing! Erase extra lines. Add details. Don't forget his hat. Shade and color.

Merry minstrel!

60

The Jester

The jester, or "fool," was an entertainer. He lived in the castle and was called on to amuse the lords and ladies. He juggled and told jokes and sang silly songs. Sometimes he carried a rattle with bells and sometimes a stick called a "slapstick." He wore gaudy clothes decorated with bells and colorful patches.

tunic

1 Start with your **basic person, front view** (see pages 5-7), but make the arms and legs bent at the elbows and knees.

2 Draw a jester's hat. Add bells to the points. Draw a tunic with a pointy bottom. Add clothing lines at the hands and feet.

3 Add hat lines. Draw a **rattle** in his left hand. Draw a line down the center of the tunic.

rattle

4 LOOK at the final drawing! Add the fun details. Shade and color. Don't forget the bells.

Index

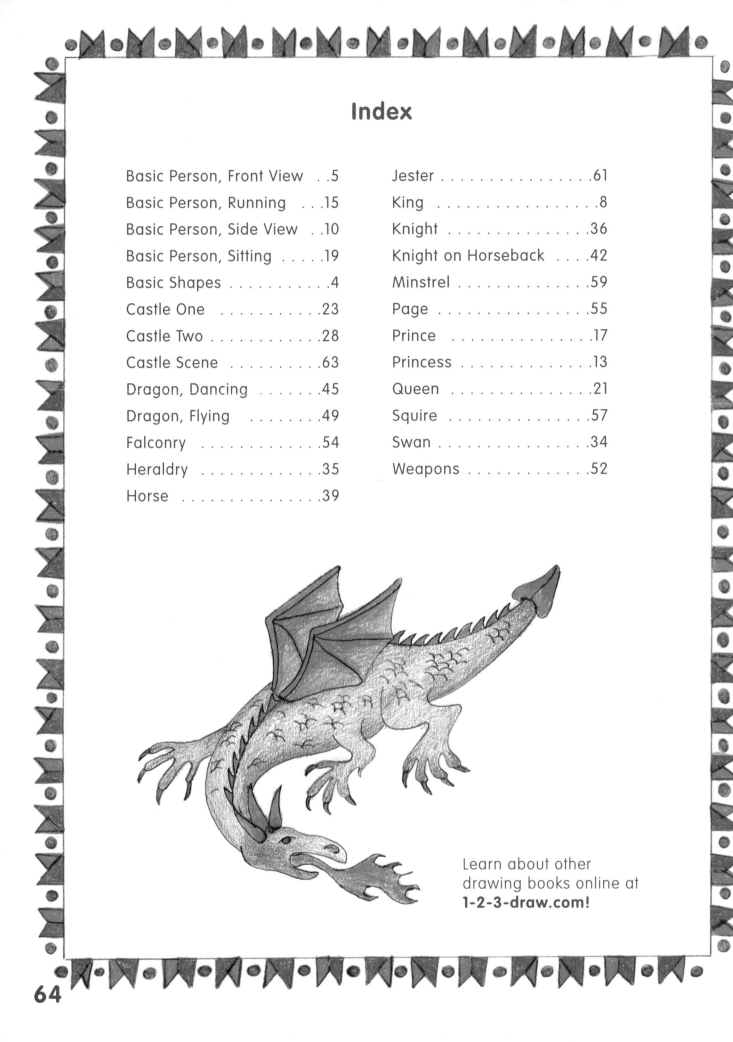

Learn about other
drawing books online at
1-2-3-draw.com!

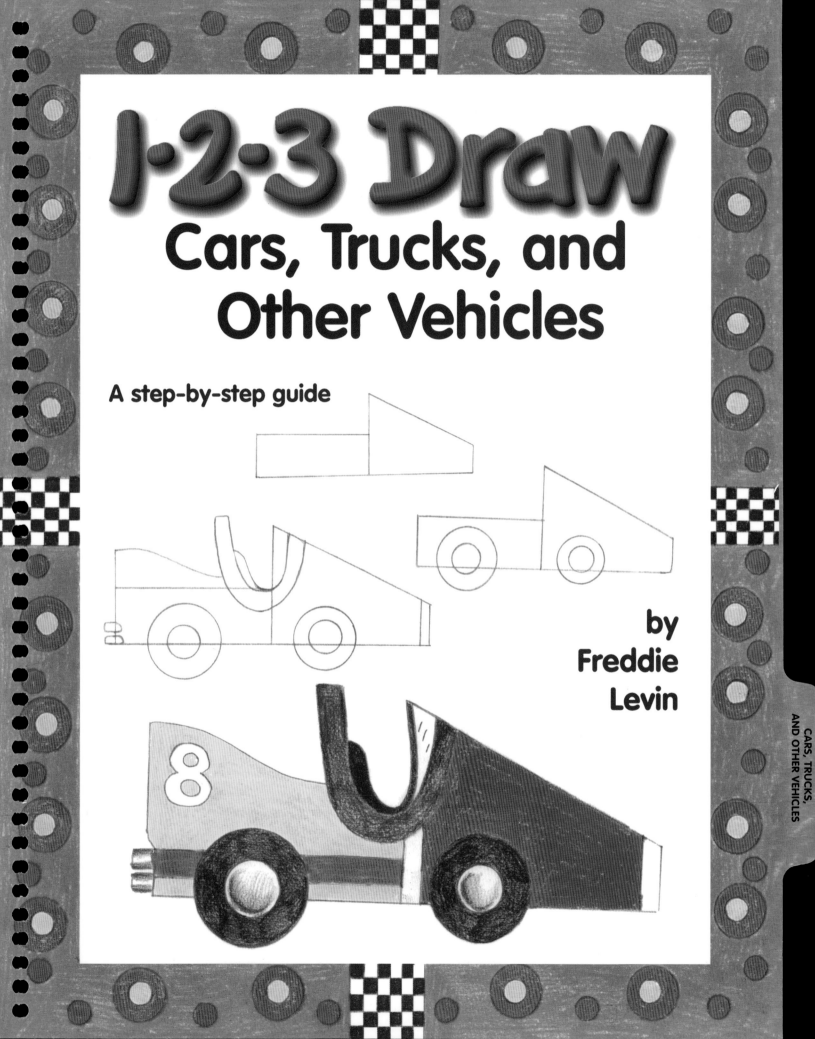

1·2·3 Draw
Cars, Trucks, and Other Vehicles

A step-by-step guide

by
Freddie
Levin

1·2·3 Draw

Cars, Trucks, and Other Vehicles

A Step-by-Step Guide

by Freddie Levin

PEEL PRODUCTIONS, INC.

Before you begin, you will need:

- a pencil
- an eraser
- a pencil sharpener
- lots of paper (recycle and reuse!)
- colored pencils
- a folder for saving work
- a comfortable place to draw
- good light
- a ruler or straight edge
- a circle template or a compass for drawing circles

Now, let's begin...!

Library of Congress Cataloging-in-Publication Data
Levin, Freddie.
   1-2-3 draw cars, trucks, and other vehicles: a step by step guide / by Freddie Levin. p.
   cm.
   Summary: Provides instructions for drawing a variety of cars, trucks, construction
   equipment and other vehicles.
   ISBN 0-939217-44-9 (pbk.)
   1. Motor vehicles in art--Juvenile literature. 2. Drawing--Technique--Juvenile literature.
   [1. Motor vehicles in art. 2. Drawing--Technique.] I. Title: One-two-three draw cars,
   trucks, and other vehicles. II. Title: Cars, trucks, and other vehicles. III. Title.

NC825.M64 L48
743'.896292--dc21   2001045839

Distributed to the trade and art
markets in North America by

NORTH LIGHT BOOKS,
an imprint of F&W Publications, Inc.
4700 East Galbraith Road
Cincinnati, OH 45236

(800) 289-0963

Contents

Important Drawing Tips

1 Draw lightly at first (SKETCH!), so you can erase extra lines.

2 Practice, practice, practice so you can get better and better!

3 Have fun drawing cars, trucks, and other vehicles!

Simple Shapes

All of the vehicles in this book are created with simple shapes.

 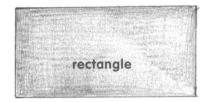

A **square** has four equal sides.

A **rectangle** has four sides; two sides are longer.

A **circle** is round. (see page 5: About drawing circles)

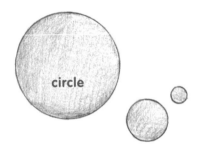

Wheels are circles. First, draw a light line to represent the ground. Then, draw the wheels touching the line.
If both wheels are touching the line, they will be even. Draw the line lightly so you can erase it later.

A **triangle** has three sides and three points. If you chop off one of the points, you have a **trapezoid**.

Drawing Circles and Lines

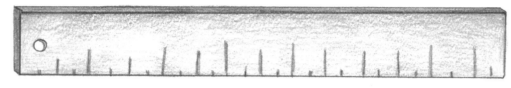

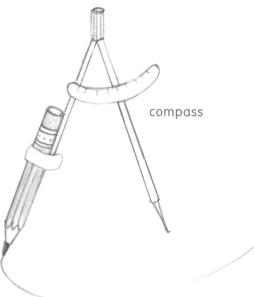

compass

Drawing circles and straight lines is hard and takes a lot of practice. To help you draw straight lines, you can use a ruler or straight edge.

To help you draw circles, you can use a **compass** or **circle template**. Both the compass and the circle template are available at art supply or office supply stores.

A **compass** is a tool with a point and a holder for a pencil. You put the point onto the paper and twirl the pencil around the point to create a circle.

A **circle template** is a plastic stencil with different size circles. You can also use coins, the bottoms of empty cups or containers, or anything you find that is round and the right size.

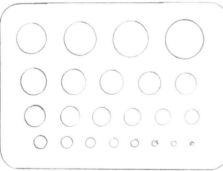

circle template

Sedan

A sedan is a four-door passenger car.
It can seat five people and has a roomy trunk.

1 Sketch a long **rectangle** to start our first car.

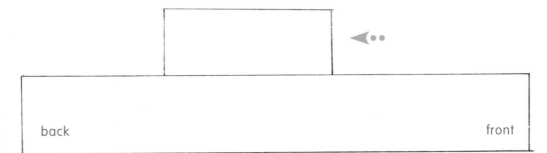

back   front

2 Draw a second **rectangle** on top of the first one. Notice that it is
not in the middle but set toward the back of the car.

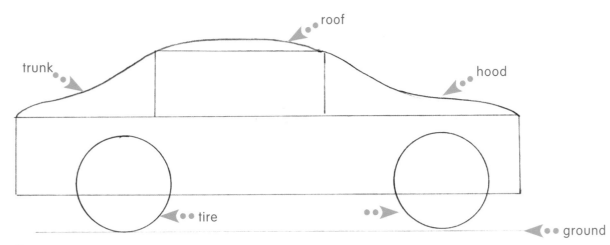

roof

trunk

hood

tire

ground

3 Draw a long curving line, using the second rectangle as your
guide, to make the trunk, roof, and hood. Draw a light line for the
ground. Draw two tires touching the line. Notice the positions of
the tires. The back tire is just to the left of the rectangle and the
front tire is closer to the front of the car.

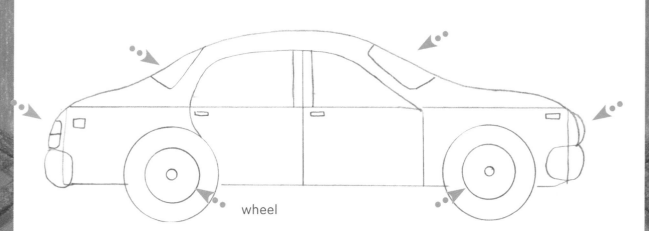

wheel

4 Draw the round back of the car. Add a bumper, a tail light and reflector. Draw the round front of the car. Add a bumper and a headlight. Draw windows, doors, and door handles. Add wheels.

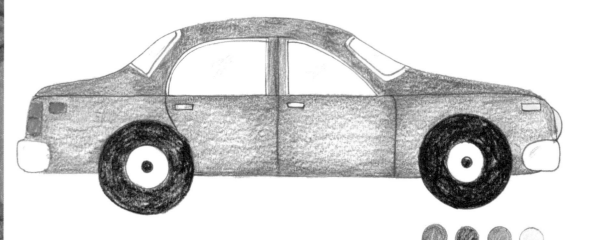

5 LOOK at the final drawing! Erase extra lines. Shade and color. Make your car any color you want!

Convertible

A convertible is a sporty car with a top that can be removed. Some convertible roofs are folded down by hand while some work automatically. Others must be removed completely. A convertible often has no back seat. It's fun to drive when the weather is nice. When it's cold or rainy, it's time to put the top up!

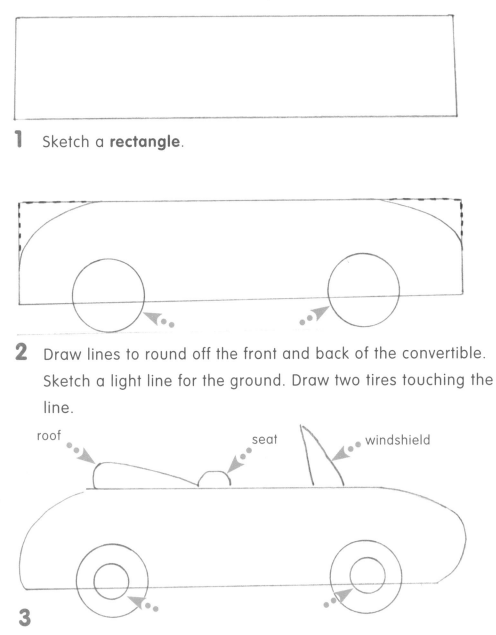

1   Sketch a **rectangle**.

2   Draw lines to round off the front and back of the convertible. Sketch a light line for the ground. Draw two tires touching the line.

roof   seat   windshield

3

Draw the folded down top of the convertible. Draw the seat just sticking up over the top line of the car. Draw the windshield. Round out the back and front of the car. Draw the wheels.

4 Add the door lines. Draw a curved line for the wheel wells.

5 On the back of the car, add a taillight and a bumper. On the front of the car, add a headlight and a bumper. Draw a door handle. Draw a line of trim along the bottom of the car.

6 LOOK at the final drawing! Erase extra lines. Shade and color your convertible a bright, sporty red.

Cool convertible!

Race Car

Race cars are shaped for speed.
The tires are big and the
whole car is low to the ground.

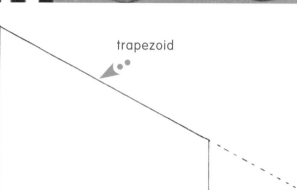

trapezoid

1 Sketch a small, thin **rectangle** and a
large **trapezoid**. (See how a **trapezoid**
is a triangle with one point cut off?)

2 Sketch a line for the ground. Draw
large tires.

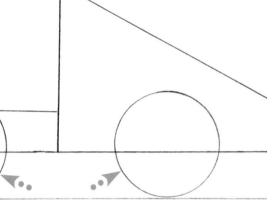

3 Draw the shape of the back of the car.
Add the wheels.

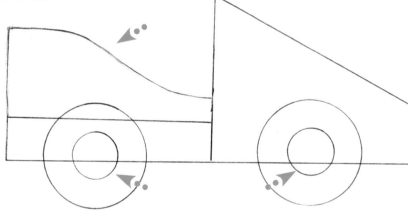

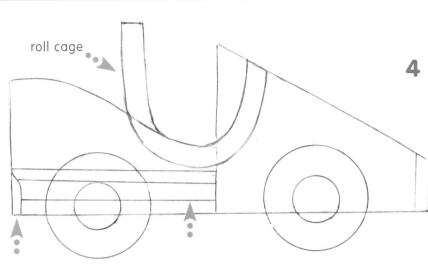

roll cage

4 Draw a "U" shape to form the roll cage (to protect the driver if the car flips). Draw two lines at an angle to make a place for the tailpipes. Add stripes along the bottom of the car. Draw a stripe at the front of the car.

5 Draw a seat for the driver. Add two tailpipes. Draw a stripe in the middle of the car underneath the windshield.

6 LOOK at the final drawing! Erase extra lines. Shade and color your race car.

Ladies and gentlemen, start your engines....

Limousine

A limousine is a long car that can carry many people. When we think of limousines, we think of rock stars and movie stars, but other people hire limousines for special events such as weddings and proms. The driver of the limousine is called a "chauffeur" (show-fer).

1 To start your limousine, sketch a long, thin **rectangle**.

2 Draw two tires.

3 Draw lines to round off the back and front of the limousine. Draw two bumpers.

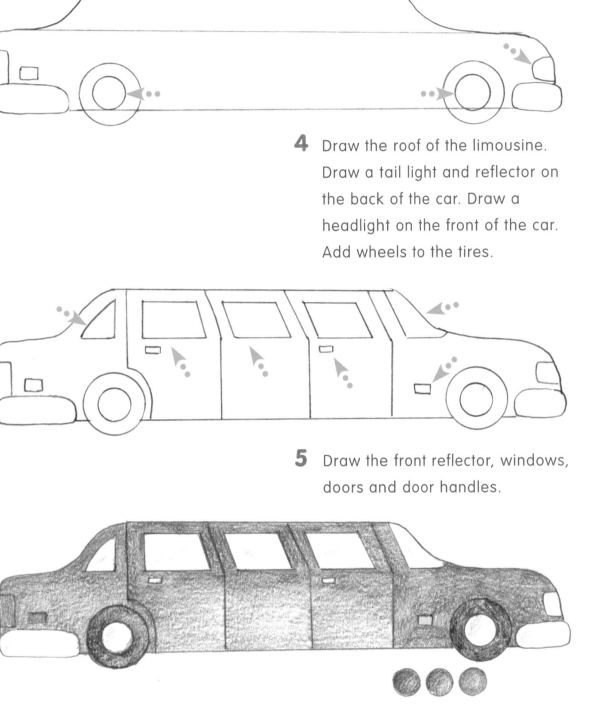

4 Draw the roof of the limousine. Draw a tail light and reflector on the back of the car. Draw a headlight on the front of the car. Add wheels to the tires.

5 Draw the front reflector, windows, doors and door handles.

6 LOOK at the final drawing! Erase extra lines. Shade and color your deluxe limo.

Old-fashioned Car

This car was made in the early 1900s. Then cars were a new invention that many people called "horseless carriages." They were slow and not very comfortable. Now cars like this are treasured by collectors and museums, and are an important part of our history.

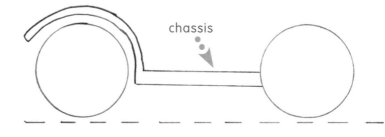

1 To start this old-fashioned car, sketch a ground line. Draw two tires on the line. Add the bottom of the chassis (cha - see) which is the frame of the car.

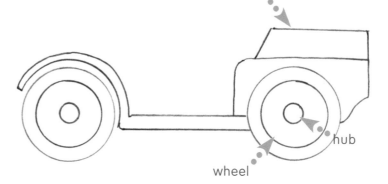

2 Add the front of the car (hood) where the motor will go. Draw the wheels and hubs.

3 On the back of the car, draw the shape for the seat and the supports for the top. On the front of the car, draw a windshield, a knob on the hood, and a head lamp.

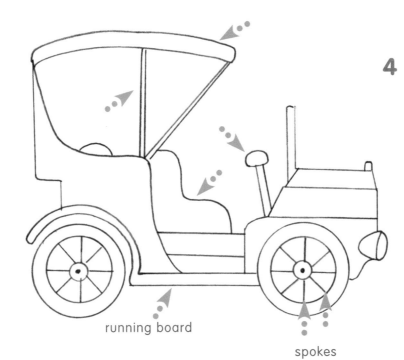

running board

spokes

4 Draw the top cover with rods for supports. Draw the seats and the platform called a "running board." Add a "steering stick." Carefully draw spokes in the wheels.

5 LOOK at the final drawing! Erase extra lines. Shade and color your old-fashioned car.

Quaint car!

Taxicab

When you need a ride and don't have a car, you can hire a taxicab. Taxi drivers take people many places. The farther the trip and the longer it takes, the more the taxi driver charges. People take cabs most often in busy downtown areas and to airports when they travel.

1 Sketch a **rectangle**.

2 Draw a long line to shape the trunk, roof, and hood.

3 Draw a roof line. Add the window and door lines. Draw two tires.

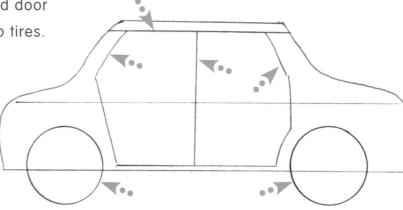

4 Draw the window and windshield lines. In the back, draw the tail light and a bumper. In the front, draw a headlight and a bumper.

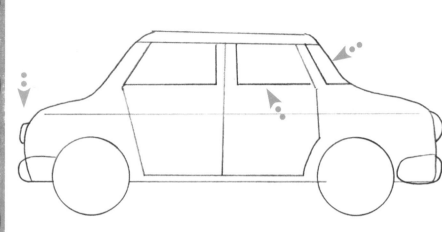

5 Put a light on top of your cab. When it's lit, it means the taxi is ready for hire. Add door handles. To decorate the cab, draw a long thin **rectangle** along the side and divide it into squares. Draw the wheels.

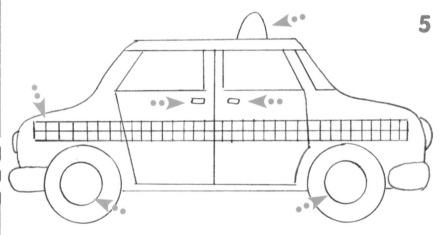

6 LOOK at the final drawing! Erase extra lines. Shade and color your taxicab.

Jeep

The Jeep was originally designed for the army during World War Two. It was a tough little vehicle that could travel on rough roads or go where there were no roads at all. No one is sure where the name Jeep came from. One guess is that it was named after a little character in a Popeye cartoon. The other guess is that it came from the initials "G.P.V." which stood for "General Purpose Vehicle."

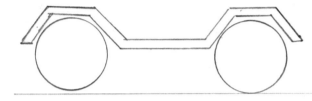

1 To start your Jeep, sketch a ground line. Draw two **circles** touching the line. Look carefully at the shape of the bottom of the chassis. It goes up, across, down, across, up, across, and down. It's a little bit like a long, stretched out "M." Draw it.

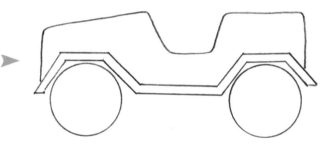

2 Draw the shape of the body. It goes up, across, down, across, up, across and down also.

3 Add a windshield. Draw a steering wheel. Add a seat.

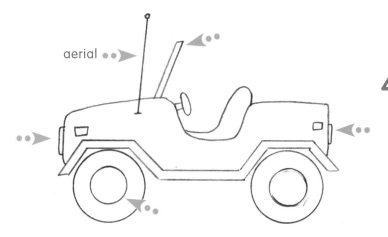

aerial

4 In the front of the Jeep, draw a headlight and a reflector. Add an aerial. In the back of the Jeep, draw a tail light and a reflector. Draw the wheels.

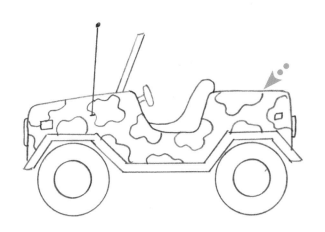

5 Add a camouflage pattern all over the Jeep. Camouflage makes the Jeep harder to see in the woods or in a field.

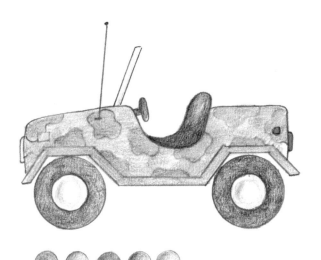

6 LOOK at the final drawing! Erase extra lines. Shade and color your Jeep.

Beetle

1 This little round car starts differently. Instead of a rectangle, it starts with a half **circle**. Sketch a half **circle**.

2 Draw the windows which are also half circles. Draw the window supports and a line for the door. Draw two curved fenders that go over the wheels.

3 Draw a door handle. Add two tires.

4 Draw a hood. Add a headlight. Draw the wheels. Finish the bottom of the fenders. Add the other door line.

5 LOOK at the final drawing! Erase extra lines. Shade and color your little round car.

My very first car was an orange Volkswagen Beetle. Since then, I have always been fond of little round cars. This one is shaped like the newer version of the Volkswagen Beetle, but all of them look like wind-up toys to me.

Invent Your Own Car

Have fun inventing some car designs of your own. Think of what you want your car to do. Do you want it to go very fast? Be extra tough? Be futuristic? Or just plain silly? Here are a few ideas to get you started.

Drawings by Daniel Levin

Drawings by Daniel Levin

Tractor-trailer or "Semi"

A tractor-trailer, sometimes called a "semi," is a really big truck. The biggest are the eighteen-wheelers. They carry all sorts of goods. The driver has a special place inside the truck to sleep on long trips.

1   Sketch a long line on the bottom. On top of the line draw a big rectangle for the trailer, and a small rectangle for the "tractor," or cab.

2   Round off the front of the cab. Draw an exhaust pipe between the cab and body.

3   Add a headlight and bumper to the front of the cab. Draw the chassis underneath the cab of the truck, connecting the front to the back. Draw two tires under the back of the truck, and two tires under the chassis at the front of the truck.

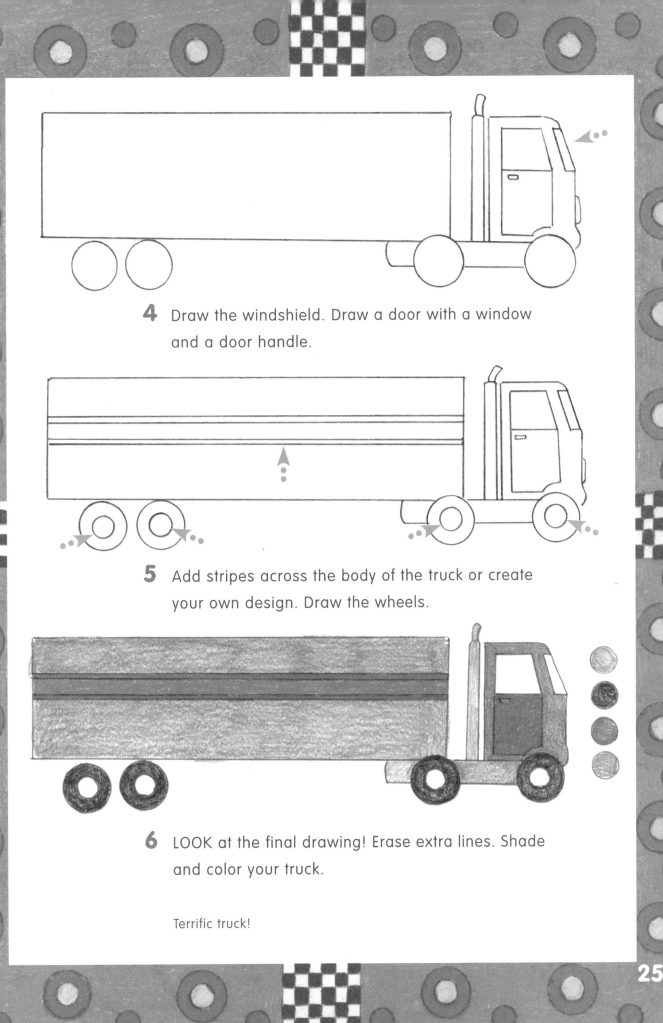

4 Draw the windshield. Draw a door with a window and a door handle.

5 Add stripes across the body of the truck or create your own design. Draw the wheels.

6 LOOK at the final drawing! Erase extra lines. Shade and color your truck.

Terrific truck!

Pick-up Truck

A pick-up truck is a smaller truck with a flat, open back. It carries smaller loads such as sacks of feed.

1 Sketch a **rectangle** to start your pick-up truck.

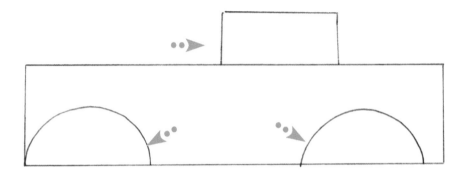

2 Add a **rectangle** on top, toward the front of the truck. Draw two half **circles** for the fenders. Notice where they are placed.

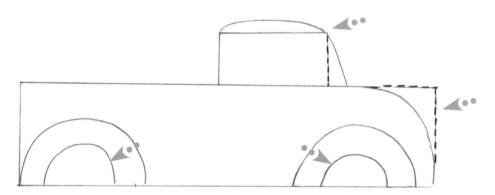

3 Draw a curving line over the top rectangle for the roof of the cab and the windshield. Draw another curved line to shape the hood of the truck. Erase the corner of the long rectangle. Draw a curved line inside the fenders.

4 Draw the windshield. Draw a door with a window and a door handle. Draw two tires and wheels underneath the fenders.

5 Draw a stripe across the body of the truck. Add a bumper, taillight, and reflector to back of the truck. Add a headlight, a reflector, and a bumper to the front of the truck.

6 LOOK at the final drawing! Erase extra lines. Shade and color your pick-up truck. What do you want to haul around? Draw it!

Tow Truck

A tow truck helps when a car breaks down or has been in an accident. A hook is placed under the front bumper of a car and a hoist lifts the car so the tow truck can pull it to a garage.

1 Sketch two **rectangles** to begin the tow truck.

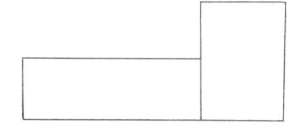

2 Draw a line to cut off the top corner of the back **rectangle**. Draw a smaller **rectangle** at the front of the tow truck and connect the corners of the two front rectangles with a line for the windshield.

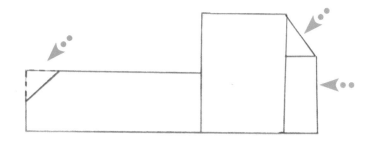

3 Add another **rectangle** and a **trapezoid** to the front of the tow truck. Draw a door with a window and a door handle.

trapezoid

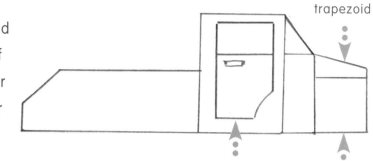

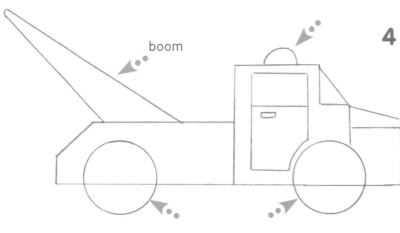

boom

4 Draw the "boom" that will raise the hook. Add the flashing light on top of the tow truck. Draw two tires.

hook

5 Add a chain and hook for towing a vehicle. Add a taillight and a reflector to the back of the truck. Add a headlight and a bumper to the front. Draw wheels.

6 LOOK at the final drawing! Erase extra lines. Shade and color your truck.

Draw a scene using a tow truck and any other car or truck you've learned to draw.

Camper

A camper is a fun way to take a driving vacation, especially with kids and pets. There are little kitchens to cook a meal, beds to sleep in, and bathrooms with showers and toilets. It's like taking a house along with you.

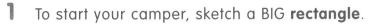

1 To start your camper, sketch a BIG **rectangle**.

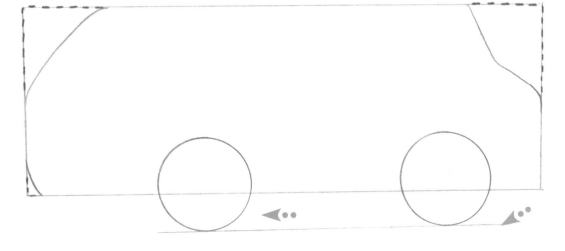

2 Draw a curving line to shape the back of the camper. Draw a curving line at the front for the hood and windshield. Sketch a line for the ground. Draw two tires touching it.

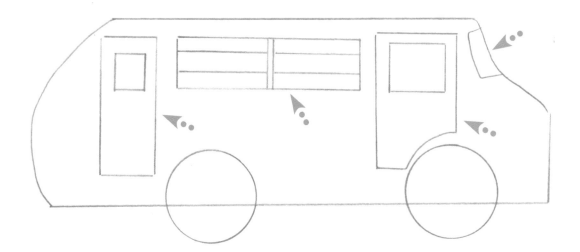

3 Draw doors at the back and front of the camper. Draw windows. Add a windshield.

4 Draw a storage box with straps on the top of the camper. Draw hand rails on the back. Add a bumper to the front.

5 Add reflectors and a taillight to the back. Add a reflector and a headlight to the front. Draw a stripe across the side of the camper. Draw the wheels.

6 LOOK at the final drawing! Erase extra lines. Shade and color your camper.

Happy trails!

Ice Cream Truck

In the summer, my favorite truck is the ice cream truck! It has freezers inside to keep ice cream cold. Sometimes the ice cream truck plays music so everyone knows it's coming.

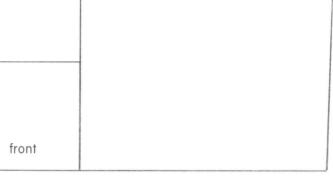

1 Sketch a big **rectangle** and a little **rectangle**. The little rectangle will be the front of truck.

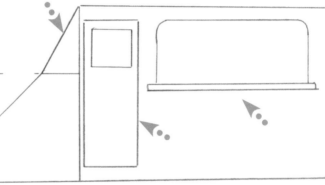

2 Above the smaller rectangle, draw a **triangle** for the windshield. Draw a line to cut off the corner of the rectangle to shape the front of the truck. Draw a door with a window. Draw a **rectangle** window in the middle of the truck with rounded top corners and a ledge underneath.

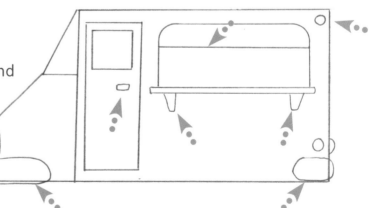

3 Add a headlight, reflector, and a bumper to the front of the truck. Draw a door handle. Draw a line for an awning over the big window. Below it, add supports for the ledge. Draw a rear bumper, reflectors, and a taillight.

4 Make a sign on top. Draw your favorite treats. Add stripes to the awning. Draw the freezers inside the truck that you can see through the window. Add a sign on the side of the truck. Draw wheels.

5 LOOK at the final drawing! Erase extra lines. Shade and color your ice cream truck.

yum!

Police Car

The police car has flashing lights and a siren to warn you to get out of the way when it is rushing to help people at the scene of a crime or an accident. Cars pull aside when they hear the siren or see the flashing light.

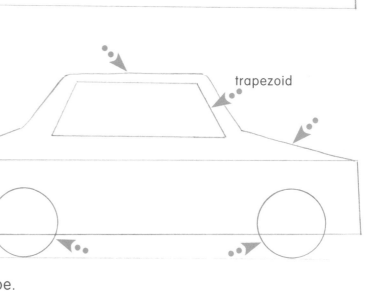

1 To start your police car, sketch a **rectangle**.

2 Draw a long line to shape the trunk, roof, and hood of the car. Draw the **trapezoid** window shape. Add two tires.

trapezoid

3 Draw the back window. Draw the windshield. Draw lines to shape the front and back doors. Add a taillight and rear bumper. Draw the headlight and front bumper.

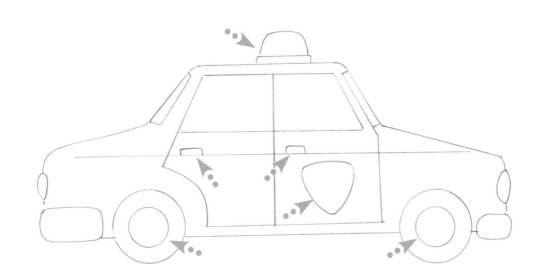

4 Add a flashing light to the top of the car. Add door handles. Draw the shield on the side of the car. Draw wheels.

5 LOOK at the final drawing! Erase extra lines. Shade and color your police car.

Mail Truck

The mail truck collects and delivers...what else? Mail! The driver collects the mail from the letter boxes and brings it to the post office to be sorted. A special sliding door on the side of the truck allows the driver to pull up to a curb and hop in and out easily.

1 Sketch a boxy **rectangle**.

2 Draw the front shape of the truck and erase the corner of the rectangle. Draw two tires.

3 Draw a door. Draw a **trapezoid** window. Add two wheels.

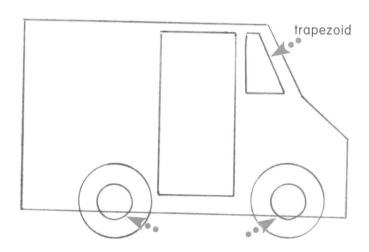

trapezoid

4 Inside the truck, draw a seat for the driver, a line for the floor, and a steering wheel. Add headlights and bumpers to the rear and front of the mail truck.

5 Draw a **rectangle** shape on the side. A poster or picture of a stamp can go here. Add three stripes across the side of the truck. Add reflectors to the front and back.

6 LOOK at the final drawing! Erase extra lines. Shade and color your mail truck.

Garbage Truck

Garbage trucks collect, haul, and dump garbage. Garbage goes into the hopper at the back of the truck. A huge blade pushes the garbage in. To empty the truck, the hopper is tipped up and the garbage is pushed out.

1 Sketch two **rectangles**.

2 Make a line for the windshield. Draw two angled lines at the back of the truck to create the hopper. Erase upper left and right corner sketch lines. Draw part of a tire under the cab. Draw two tires to support the back of the truck.

3 Add two vertical lines to the cab for the window and door. Draw a fender over the front tire. Add wheels to the tires.

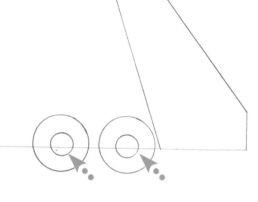

4 Draw a flashing light on the top of the cab. Draw a windshield, a side window, and a door handle. Add a headlight, reflector, and front bumper. On the side of the truck, draw the three shapes you see. Draw the lines on the side of the hopper. Add reflectors and a taillight to the back of the truck.

5 LOOK at the final drawing! Erase extra lines. Shade and color your garbage truck.

Great garbage truck!

School Bus

This school bus takes many children to school at the same time. Some school buses have lifts so that kids in wheelchairs can ride the bus. When a school bus loads or unloads children, a special stop sign pops out of the side of the bus to let other drivers know they must stop too.

1 Sketch a **rectangle**.

2 Draw a roof on top of the bus. Draw two vertical lines at the front of the bus. These will be doors. Add the **trapezoid** shape of the windshield to the front of the bus.

trapezoid

3 Draw the windows. Add a stripe to the side of the bus. Add windows to the doors.

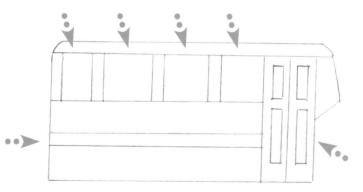

4 Add lights to the roof of the bus. Draw tail lights and a rear bumper. Draw the hood and fender over the front tire to shape the front of the bus. Add a headlight and a front bumper.

5 Draw two tires and wheels.

6 LOOK at the final drawing! Erase extra lines. Shade and color your school bus.

Super school bus!

Ambulance

An ambulance rushes to the hospital, carrying people who are sick or injured. In the back of the truck, paramedics give first aid. The ambulance has a loud siren and flashing lights to warn other cars to pull over. The ambulance driver knows every minute counts when someone needs help.

1 Sketch three **rectangles**: one large, one medium, and one small.

2 Draw a line to cut off the corner of the middle rectangle for the windshield. Draw a line to cut off the corner of the smallest rectangle to shape the hood. Draw two tires.

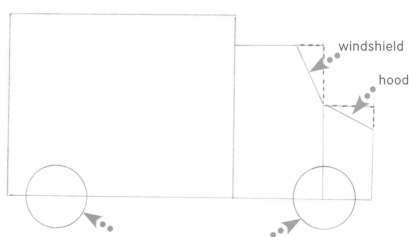

windshield

hood

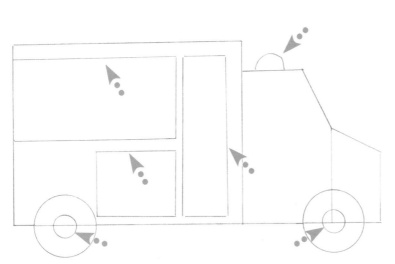

3 Add a flashing light to the top of the cab. Draw **rectangles** on the side of the ambulance for storage compartments. Draw two wheels.

4 Draw a door with a window.

5 Draw reflectors, headlights, tail lights, and bumpers. Draw the door handle. Sketch two **rectangles** to make the red cross on the side of the ambulance. This shows it is a medical vehicle. Draw handles on two of the storage compartments.

6 LOOK at the final drawing! Erase extra lines. Shade and color your ambulance.

Awesome ambulance!

Fire Truck

Fire trucks also have flashing lights and sirens. Every second counts in putting out fires and saving people's lives.There are several different kinds of fire trucks. Some pump water and some have ladders to reach high to the tops of burning buildings. Some fire trucks carry their own water and some have hoses that attach to fire hydrants.

cab

1 Sketch a line for the ground. Make it light so that you can erase it later. Draw a long, low **rectangle** and a **square** for the cab of the truck.

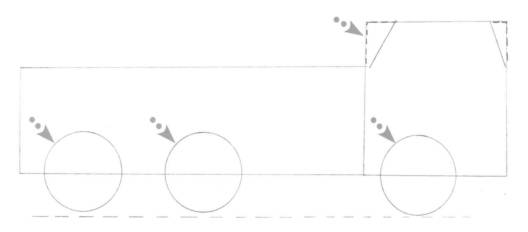

2 Draw lines to shape the top corners of the cab. Add three tires. Notice where the tires are placed. One is under the cab and two are toward the back of the fire truck.

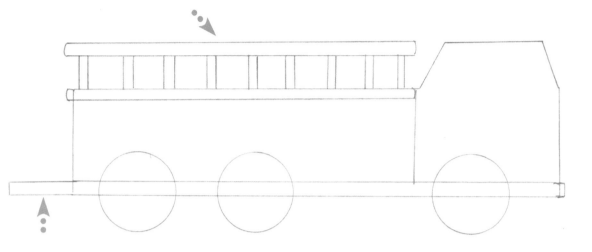

3 Draw a ladder along the back of the fire truck. Draw a long thin **rectangle** along the bottom of the fire truck. It sticks out the back. It will be a place for a fire fighter to stand.

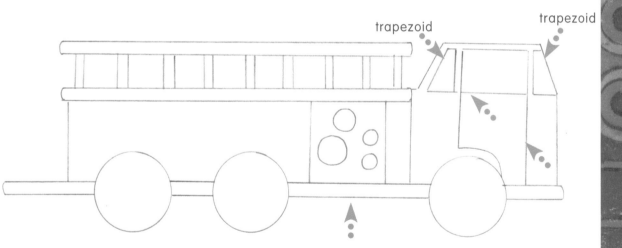

trapezoid

trapezoid

4 Draw **trapezoids** for the windows. Draw a door with a window on the cab. Draw a **square** with **circles** in it. They will be pressure gauges and valves to connect hoses.

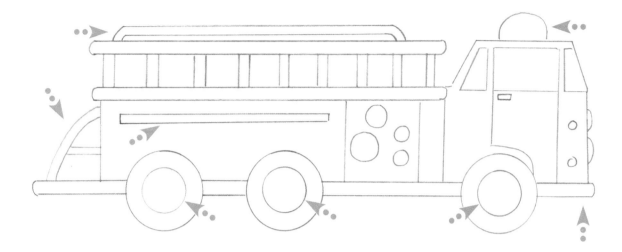

5 Add a flashing light to the top of the cab. Add headlights and reflectors to the front of the cab. Draw a rail at the top of the fire truck above the ladder. Draw hand rails at the back of the fire truck. Draw wheels.

6 LOOK at the final drawing! Erase extra lines. Shade and color your fire truck.

Bookmobile

The bookmobile is a small traveling library. It takes a selection of books to people who cannot get to the library. They borrow the books until the next time the bookmobile is in their neighborhood. A librarian helps them find what they want. Next to the ice cream truck, the bookmobile is my favorite!

1 Sketch a **rectangle**.

2 Look carefully at the shape of the front of the bookmobile. Draw it.

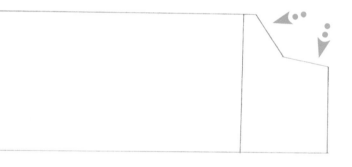

3 Sketch a light line for the ground. Draw two tires.

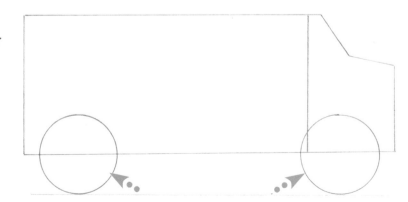

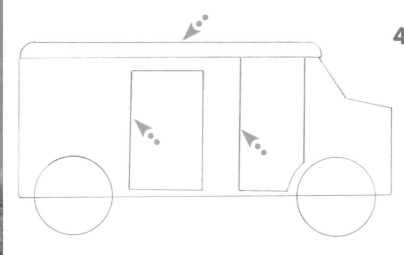

4 Draw a line for the roof. Draw a door at the front for the driver. Add a sliding door to the middle of the bookmobile.

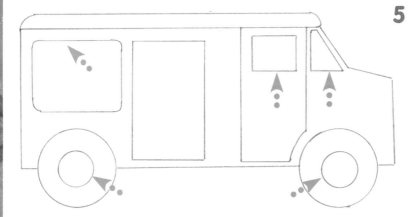

5 Add windows. Draw a **rectangle** sign with rounded corners on the back side. Draw wheels.

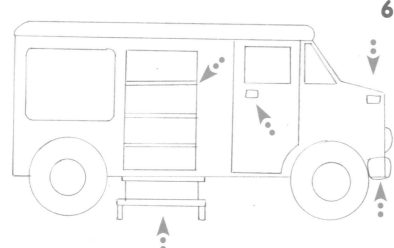

6 Draw a front headlight, reflector and bumper. Add a door handle to the driver's door. Draw shelves inside the bookmobile. Draw steps under the door.

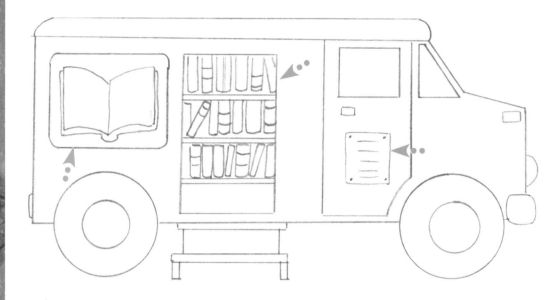

7 Draw a sign on the driver's door telling the schedule. Draw books on the shelves inside the bookmobile. Draw an open book on the sign on the side of the bookmobile.

8 LOOK at the final drawing! Erase extra lines. Shade and color your bookmobile.

Cement Truck

At the building site, workers dig the foundation for a building. When the ground is ready, the cement truck comes. The drum on the back of the truck rolls so the wet cement won't set. Wet cement is emptied into the ground through a chute. It has to be done all at once so the foundation will be strong and won't crack.

1 Sketch an upright **rectangle** for the cab and a long thin **rectangle** for the chassis of the truck.

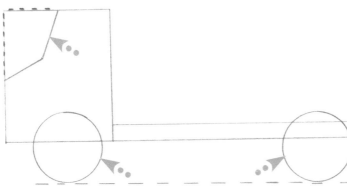

2 Draw lines for the windshield and hood of the cab. Erase the corner of the rectangle. Sketch a line for the ground. Draw three tires. Notice where they are placed.

3 Draw a **rectangle** on an angle.

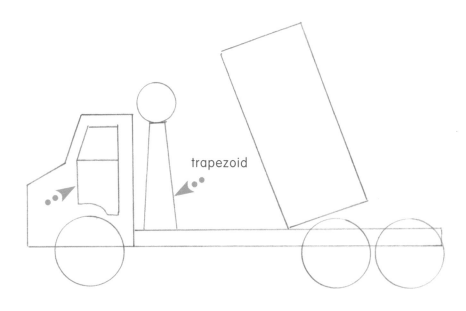

trapezoid

4 Draw a door and window on the cab of the truck. Behind the cab, draw a **trapezoid** topped by a **circle**, the support for the drum.

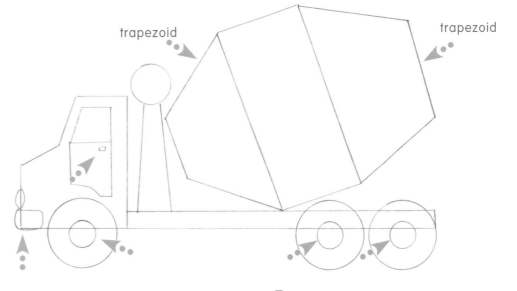

trapezoid   trapezoid

5 Draw a headlight and bumper on the front of the cab. Add a handle to the door. To complete the drum, draw a **trapezoid** on either side of the **rectangle**. Draw the wheels.

6 LOOK at the final drawing! Erase extra lines. Shade and color your cement truck.

Bulldozer

Bulldozers come in many sizes. A fairly little one like this is useful because it can turn around and maneuver in small spaces. It can push and lift stones and rubble. It has crawler treads over its wheels to help it move over bumpy ground.

1 Sketch a big and a small **rectangle** with a little space between them. Draw three wheels.

2 Draw a line for the windshield. Erase the corner of the **rectangle**. Add a door with a **trapezoid** window and a handle on the cab of the bulldozer. Draw an exhaust pipe on the top of the smaller **rectangle**. Draw a vent on the side of the smaller **rectangle**. Draw three wheels.

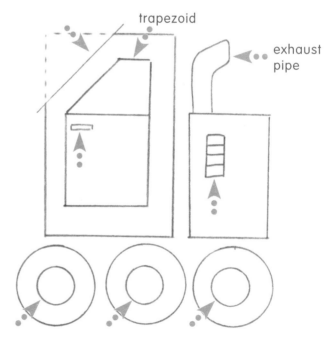

trapezoid

exhaust pipe

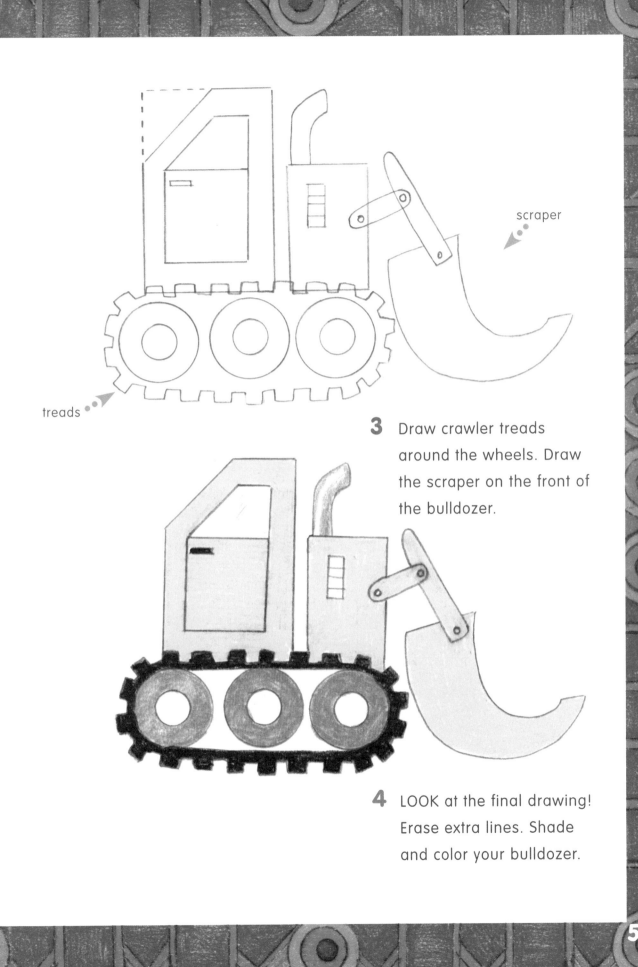

scraper

treads

3 Draw crawler treads around the wheels. Draw the scraper on the front of the bulldozer.

4 LOOK at the final drawing! Erase extra lines. Shade and color your bulldozer.

Back Hoe

A back hoe is a great digger. It has a bucket on the front with teeth to cut into the ground. It makes holes for the foundations of buildings.

1 Sketch a **rectangle**. Draw a line to cut off a corner of the rectangle and erase the point.

trapezoid

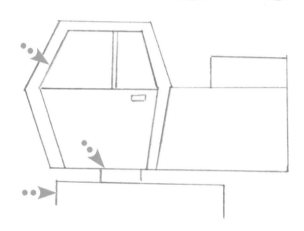

2 Draw a **trapezoid** and a small **rectangle** on top of the first **rectangle**.

3 Draw windows and a door on the cab. Under the door, draw a small **rectangle**. Notice its position. Start a **rectangle** under that, but don't finish the bottom yet.

4 Draw three wheels. Draw a line around the wheels to begin the treads.

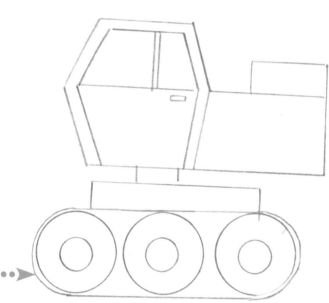

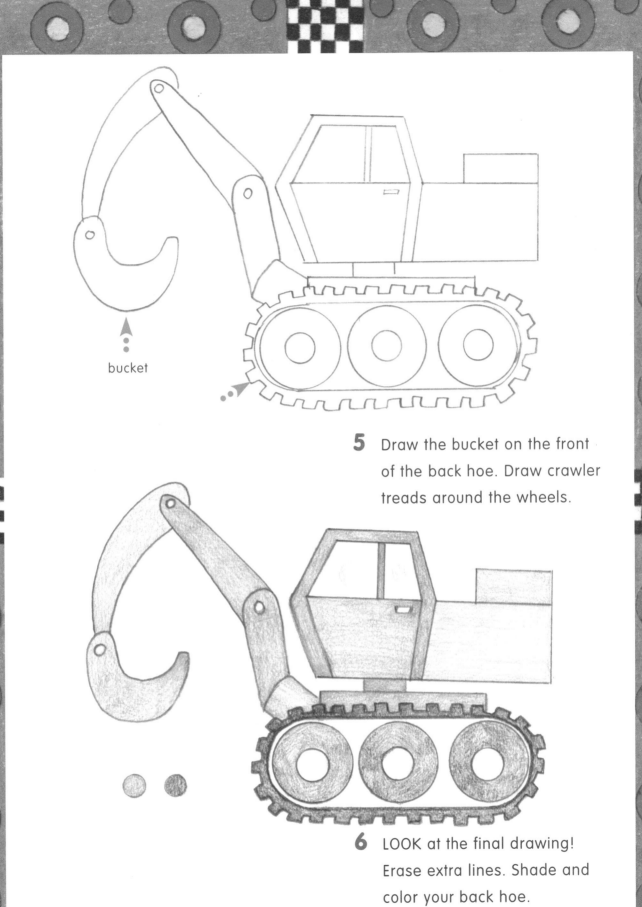

5 Draw the bucket on the front of the back hoe. Draw crawler treads around the wheels.

bucket

6 LOOK at the final drawing! Erase extra lines. Shade and color your back hoe.

Dump Truck

A dump truck is a big truck with a giant box on the back. It hauls stones and dirt away from a construction site and it dumps dirt and gravel where it is needed to fill in holes. The box on the back of the truck is lifted by a hydraulic (hi-draw-lik) shaft. The back of the truck opens to dump its load.

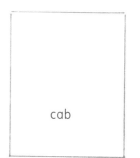

1 Sketch two **rectangles**. The smaller, upright rectangle will be the cab of the truck. The large tipped up rectangle will be the back of the truck. Notice the angle.

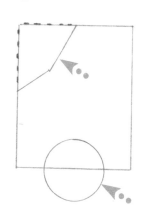

2 Draw lines for the windshield and hood of the cab. Erase the corner of the **rectangle**. Draw three tires. One is under the cab. Two more are under the back of the truck.

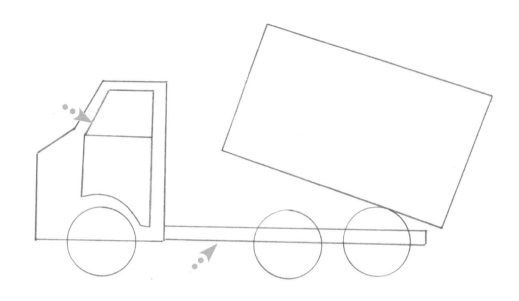

3 Draw a long, thin **rectangle** for the chassis of the truck Add the door and window on the cab.

lift

4 Draw the hydraulic lift. Draw an inner **rectangle** inside the box of the truck. Draw the wheels.

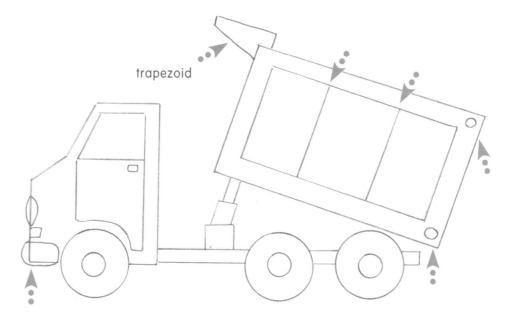

trapezoid

5 Add a headlight, reflector, and bumper to the cab. Draw a **trapezoid** on the upper left hand corner of the box. Divide the inner **rectangle** with two vertical lines. Add reflectors to the back of the truck.

6 LOOK at the final drawing! Erase extra lines. Shade and color your dump truck.

Have fun drawing machines at your own construction site!

Index

Learn about other drawing books online at **1-2-3-draw.com!**

1·2·3 Draw
DRAWING PAPER